W9-BCK-636

Violence in Schools

VIOLENCE IN SCHOOLS

Issues, Consequences, and Expressions

Edited by Kathy Sexton-Radek

Foreword by Robert Schleser

Westport, Connecticut
London

Library of Congress Cataloging-in-Publication Data

Violence in schools : issues, consequences, and expressions / edited by Kathy Sexton-Radek; foreword by Robert Schleser.

    p. cm.

  Includes bibliographical references and index.

  ISBN 0–275–97987–3 (alk. paper)

  1. School violence—Psychological aspects. 2. School violence—Prevention. 3. School psychology. I. Sexton-Radek, Kathy.

LB3013.3.V57 2005

371.7′82—dc22   2004007228

British Library Cataloguing in Publication Data is available.

Copyright © 2005 by Kathy Sexton-Radek

All rights reserved. No portion of this book may be reproduced, by any process or technique, without the express written consent of the publisher.

Library of Congress Catalog Card Number: 2004007228

ISBN: 0–275–97987–3

First published in 2005

Praeger Publishers, 88 Post Road West, Westport, CT 06881

An imprint of Greenwood Publishing Group, Inc.

www.praeger.com

Printed in the United States of America

The paper used in this book complies with the Permanent Paper Standard issued by the National Information Standards Organization (Z39.48–1984).

10 9 8 7 6 5 4 3 2 1

CONTENTS

Foreword   vii
    Dr. Robert Schleser

Preface   ix

Acknowledgments   xi

I.   **THINKING ABOUT VIOLENCE**
       PREVENTION PROGRAMMING   1

1.   Theoretical Foundation   3
       Mary Lawson

2.   Psychoanalytic/Developmental Theories Related to
       Adolescence and Aggression   35
       Charles E. Goldsmith

3.   Cognitive Perspective to Violence Expression 49
       Korrie Allen

4.   Psychopathological and Psychosocial Factors That
       Contribute to Violent Behavior in Youth   73
       Patrice Paul

II. **ENACTING VIOLENCE PREVENTION PROGRAMMING** 89

5. The Teaching of Violence Prevention in a School Setting—What Can Be Done? 91
Rene Pichler, Amanda Urban, and Lynda Bockewitz

6. Individualized Therapy Approaches: Victim's Focus 103
Theresa Risolo and Amy C. Patella

7. Bullying and Aggression among Youth 121
James Galezewski

8. Forensic Issues and Violence Prevention Programming 145
Julia M. Klco

III. **BEHAVIOR EXPRESSIONS AND VIOLENCE PREVENTION PROGRAMMING** 155

9. Research Issues Related to Conflict Resolution Intervention Programs 157
Kathy Sexton-Radek

Afterword 175

Appendix I: Web Resources for Violence Prevention Programming 177

Appendix II: Case Study: Self-Perception of Anger Conflict Resolution Intervention at a Chicago Inner-City School—Fourth-Graders 179

Glossary 181

Bibliography 183

Index 185

About the Editor and the Contributors 189

FOREWORD

Violence in schools, from simple bullying to murder, is increasing. The statistics reported in this book are staggering. Dr. Korrie Allen reports that 84 percent of junior high school students report experiencing at least one incident of bullying or teasing. Rene Pichler and Amanda Urban report that there have been over 250 school deaths attributable to violent behavior since 1992. Clearly, there is an urgent need for a lucid, in-depth discussion of school violence and how to prevent it.

Dr. Kathy Sexton-Radek has compiled an impressive group of authors, including both academicians and practitioners. Overall, they present a comprehensive view of the many different types of school violence and means for preventing it. This book will serve as an important resource for teachers, counselors, school administrators, and psychologists working with violent children and their victims.

The book is divided into three major parts. The first part provides a conceptual foundation for understanding school violence. Dr. Mary Lawson presents an ecological-developmental model that helps the reader understand the sociocultural context in which violence occurs. Rev. Dr. Charles E. Goldsmith presents a more traditional model, which focuses on the development of aggression in the individual. Dr. Korrie Allen presents a cognitive perspective that addresses bullying and teasing, which are vastly more pervasive than actual physical violence but equally devastating to the victim. Finally, Dr. Patrice Paul reviews the *Diagnostic and Statistical Manual of Mental Disorders*

(4th ed.; DSM-IV) diagnostic categories associated with violent behavior and explores the relationship between psychopathology and violence.

The second part presents programmatic strategies for the prevention of violence. Dr. Rene Pichler, Dr. Amanda Urban, and Lynda Bockewitz present teacher-friendly approaches, including one that incorporates pairing less socially skilled children with more socially skilled children to teach conflict resolution skills and create an environment of peace. Dr. Theresa Risolo and Amy C. Patella focus on the psychological consequences of being bullied and bullying. Dr. James Galezewski discusses the "phenomena of bullying" and identifies the biological, cognitive, and social bases of aggression. His give in-depth coverage of parenting style and the role of parenting in violent behavior. Dr. Julia M. Klco offers several case studies on violent mentally ill children. She suggests the need for individual treatment and increased funding for violence prevention programs.

The third part includes the final chapter, by editor Dr. Kathy Sexton-Radek, that reviews methodological issues in research on conflict resolution programs. She focuses on the complexity of predicting violence and evaluating the efficacy of conflict resolution programs, which appears to be a daunting but essential task.

The deaths of one-third of all children, adolescents, and young adults can be attributed to violence. As the statistics in this book indicate, violence is increasing. Perpetrators and victims are younger and younger, and their behavior is more lethal. I think you may be shocked by the picture of violence in our schools described in this book. School should be a place for children to learn and grow socially competent. School should be peaceful. This book will not end violence in the schools, but it is a beginning. It presents a grim reality, but also offers suggestions for a better future for our children.

Dr. Robert Schleser
Institute for Psychology
Illinois Institute of Technology
Chicago, Illinois

PREFACE

The concept for this book emerged from eight years' experience with conflict resolution training in the inner-city public schools of Chicago. My learning and insights, while forwarded by the knowledge of the literature, developed from observation and admiration of "touch-stone" teachers such as Mr. Baier and Mr. Ihles of Hancock Academy and Lynda Slimmer of the University of Illinois, Chicago. The understanding of youth behavior is a difficult one. These master teachers, along with the constructive commentaries from all my students, taught me the realities of this world. I am indebted to them.

This work is a logical, theoretically focused product of talented scientist practitioners who possess the compassion to connect with troubled youth and the clinical acumen to effectively assist them in life. The three parts of the book provide the reader with a sequence of how to think about these issues, what to expect from programming, and what to anticipate from participants (youth) of violence prevention programming.

ACKNOWLEDGMENTS

The editor wishes to thank her sons Brett, Neal, and Ted for their patience with their mom as she worked on this project and went to other kids' schools over the years to be of some help. The editor also wishes to thank Peggy Dumas for her perfect word processing of this document.

The authors of chapter 6, Theresa Risolo and Amy Patella, wish to thank Erika Fromm for her helpful advisory comments in reading this manuscript. The field of psychology, while advanced by voluminous writings and teachings of Erika Fromm, mourns the recent death of this conceptual leader and educator.

Part I

THINKING ABOUT VIOLENCE PREVENTION PROGRAMMING

Chapter 1

THEORETICAL FOUNDATION

Mary Lawson

INTRODUCTION

Eminent violence researchers Garbarino, Kostelny, and Dubrow (1991a, 1991b) ask us to recognize that children in America's violence-saturated urban environments are growing up in war zones; Garbarino and his colleagues then remind us of the 1960s antiwar slogan, "War is not good for children and other living things." Children and violence don't mix—that's what we'd like to believe, at least. Children should *not* be the victims of serious physical force intended to injure, damage, or intimidate them: they deserve better and we adults rightly feel obliged to give it to them. Perhaps even more appalling than encountering a child victim is contemplating the child who is a determined perpetrator of violence. In recent years, we have all had that experience. Two teenagers roam throughout a suburban high school killing indiscriminately. Two young boys drop an even younger child to his death from the window of a high-rise. Their acts and the age seem incongruous. How did they get so vicious so soon?

Yet a look at a few statistics tells us that despite our wishes, violence and youth do mix; they have an affinity that is impossible to deny. The onset of criminal violence is greatest between ages 14 and 16, while its prevalence peaks between ages 15 and 19 (Loeber & Stouthamer-Loeber, 1998a; Williams, Guerra, & Elliott, 1997). For most perpetrators, their involvement will be short lived (from 1 to 3 years); they will be in their late teens or early twenties when they desist.

Since those committing violent acts often choose their age peers as victims, victimization is also disproportionately inflicted on youth. Based on figures from the National Crime Victimization Survey, Macmillan (2001) notes that the risk of being victimized reaches its peak in adolescence, slowly declines in early adulthood, and then takes a plunge. An adolescent is 23 times more likely to be assaulted than is an elder.

While this overall pattern of age-related victimization and perpetration is not new, it is worth noting some changes that support our impression that the problem of youth violence is getting worse. First is the increased lethality of violence involving youth (Fraser, 1996), with homicide becoming the second leading cause of death among adolescents. While the incidence of homicide from 1976 to 1995 remained constant or even declined overall, there was a dramatic increase in homicides committed by adolescent males. African American males were disproportionately involved, both as perpetrators and victims. At the same time, the use of handguns in the commission of homicides increased dramatically; the involvement of drugs in homicides also jumped sharply (Williams et al., 1997).

The second change is the increased participation of younger adolescents (12- to 14-year-olds) in the more serious forms of violence (Reppucci, Wollard, & Fried, 1999; Williams et al., 1997). Again, the widespread availability of handguns—the great "levelers" in conflict situations—may have contributed to this trend, encouraging younger and smaller adolescents to feel emboldened to participate in activities leading to violent outcomes.

While lethal attacks within or near schools capture public attention, officials are quick to point out that schools are relatively safe contexts for children, compared with homes or neighborhoods. Although it is true that schools are less dangerous than other environments, they cannot be counted on to be safe havens (Astor, Pitner, & Duncan, 1996; Osofsky & Osofsky, 2001). And teenagers often perceive them as being *less* safe than these other, more dangerous locales (Elliott, Hamburg, & Williams, 1998). They see their schools as becoming more violent. One study, for example, revealed that over half of teenagers experienced concern about being physically attacked in or around school (Harris and Associates, 1993). The disconnect between crime statistics and adolescents' perceptions may stem from the invisibility to authorities of much of students' victimization. Research drawing information directly from students reveals much higher rates of victimization than reported in official records (Elliott et al., 1998).

The concentration of violent offending within a fairly narrow age range and our awareness that involvement in violence has the potential to derail movement toward developmental goals, suggest that we adopt a developmental perspective when considering prevention options. Involvement is violence is both a manifestation and a distortion of some so-called normal developmental trends during this period of childhood and adolescence. The next section explores several aspects of this relationship.

AGGRESSION FROM INFANCY THROUGH ADOLESCENCE

Violence is the threat or use of physical force that causes physical injury, damage, or intimidation of another person. Aggression is a broader concept, involving efforts to harm or control another person. Some forms of aggression employ physical force while others do not, and some forms seem less concerned with harming than with controlling another person. Aggression, but not violence, is manifested quite early in childhood; it then typically undergoes changes in its forms and functions. For a minority of individuals, these changes culminate in a pattern of violent acts of long duration. However, most children take other routes, learning to manage aggressive impulses in essentially nonviolent ways or perhaps experimenting with violence during the period of adolescence.

The expression of anger and attempts to retaliate can be seen in infancy. In the middle of the first year, the infant develops a rudimentary sense of cause-and-effect relationships. With this change, infants become capable of being frustrated by circumstances that block their wishes. Frustration leads to anger. Protest or striking out at the perceived source of frustration may follow. Boys are likely to display anger more than girls because they are more emotionally labile and less able to regulate their emotional states without input from their caregivers (Loeber & Hay, 1997). In general, infants and toddlers show substantial gains in their ability to modulate and manage the negative emotions that might lead to aggression. The infant-caregiver *attachment system* is thought to be influential in this change for both males and females (Masten & Coatsworth, 1998).

As they move into toddlerhood, children face a variety of situations that involve frustration and conflict. The classic, full-blown temper tantrum is a manifestation of their displeasure. On the whole, aggressive or resistive behavior does not dominate social interaction. Most of the aggression is *instrumental* rather than *hostile*. It aims to fix a situation rather than hurt a person, and it tends to emerge relatively late in a dispute (Loeber & Hay, 1997). The toddler grabs a toy or shoves another child away from a desired object. Few gender differences are shown in this kind of aggression.

Throughout the preschool and early school years, instrumental aggression declines, as children become more capable of negotiating conflict over objects with words and are repeatedly instructed to do so. Boys lag girls during this period in their abandonment of instrumental aggression, perhaps because of their slower language development.

As instrumental aggression is declining, other manifestations of aggression appear. Hostile aggression, which involves an intention to hurt or damage another person, is on the rise. It can be physical or social, overt or covert. Boys appear to be more physically aggressive than girls, although this perception may reflect girls' greater tendency to hide their physical aggression and bullying. Girls also seem to specialize in an often covert form of social hostility called *relational aggression,* which involves trying to harm another person's social relationships or reputation.

Although most girls and boys show a decrease in peer-directed aggression from early through middle childhood, they may continue to be physically and verbally aggressive with their siblings during this time. Such sibling interactions are not predictive of maladjustment outside the family, unless they are unusually frequent or intense (Loeber & Hay, 1997).

A subgroup of boys fails to show this drop-off in aggression during the early school years. When continued aggression is combined with cruelty to other children and cruelty to animals (symptoms of a conduct disorder), the likelihood of progression to other, more serious forms of aggression is increased (Loeber & Hay, 1997).

Not all aggression in childhood emerges from conflict, of course. Some derives from status- or dominance-striving. Rough-and-tumble play from early childhood on may help to establish dominance hierarchies, especially among males. In early childhood these episodes of roughhousing offer an opportunity to cement friendship as well as improve fighting skills. The reversibility of roles (dominance and submission) helps to keep the interaction fun for both parties, even as they both become aware of who is likely to win any serious contest for dominance.

As children move toward and through adolescence, their aggression takes on different manifestations and functions. Adolescents' self-absorption and prickly sensitivity to the views of others means that acceptance by a peer group takes on increased importance, as does their own position within the status hierarchy of that group. In addition, adolescence is a period when transitions to larger, more complex social environments take place (e.g., enrollment in high school). These settings may involve greater diversity and competition than the adolescent previously encountered.

When the social order is in flux, it may seem necessary to fight to establish a reputation. Rough-and-tumble play reemerges with an edge. It can quickly shade into serious fighting, as physical prowess becomes a way to stake a claim to dominance within the group or, if the word spreads, within the larger adolescent community (Fagan & Wilkinson, 1998).

Once established, adolescent peer groups may turn their attention to *collective* forms of aggression, to meet a variety of instrumental and status-related ends. Peer group members are often similar to each other in levels of antisocial tendencies. Children, especially boys, who show high levels of aggressive interactions with their peers in early or middle childhood, are likely to be rejected by most of their peers and excluded from most peer groups. These outcasts gravitate toward each other and form associations that reinforce their individual antisocial tendencies. They frequently fight with each other but eventually band together to victimize outsiders. Through this process, a delinquent peer group is born. With increased organization, symbolic expression (e.g., dress codes, hand symbols, and insignia), and a territorial base, a peer group becomes a gang.

All peer groups recognizable to others can provide an identity latch for their members, one reason for their extraordinary appeal during adolescence, when identity concerns are paramount. For many peer groups, especially gangs, the collective identity revolves around violence as well as excessive displays of masculine stereotyped behavior (Fagan & Wilkinson, 1998).

Even adolescents who are not gang members might seek to employ violence and the adoption of *street style* to gain some of the impression management benefits that gang members enjoy. In communities that offer their youth few avenues to the kinds of social status and roles available to adolescents in other contexts, toughness may be one of the only dimensions in which a person can seek to rise. In such communities, there may be a nearly constant threat of danger from individuals who are trying to rise in the status hierarchy through fighting or who are overly reactive to signs of disrespect (Baumeister, Smart, & Boden, 1996). A reputation for toughness and an embrace of certain elements of street style may protect even an unaffiliated male, which Fagan and Wilkinson (1998) described as a deterrent value to ward off attacks from other males. Even females in these settings may cultivate a reputation for toughness or so-called heart in order to keep other females away from their boyfriends and deter attacks by males or other females (Fagan & Wilkinson, 1998).

For the most part, females' status claims and their attempts to resolve conflicts become less likely to employ violence as they move through adolescence. However, males continue to be involved in violent confrontations during this period (Loeber & Hay, 1997).

These are many other potential uses of violence that appeal to adolescents, especially disaffected ones: defiance of authority, pursuit of material goods, the domination involved in taking possessions from another or from rape, retribution, the thrill of risk taking, or the expression of a type of artist/deviant (Fagan & Wilkinson, 1998). The upturn in violence during this developmental stage suggests that the various uses of violence appeal to many adolescents. Yet it is also obvious that much of the time adolescents meet their developmental needs for belonging, status, identity, and independence without resorting to violence. Further, those who experiment with violence during this period often seem to readily leave it behind. Improvements in cognition and impulse control may play a part in this process, as does movement into the adult's roles of work, marriage, and parenthood (Loeber & Hay, 1997).

DEVELOPMENTAL PATHWAYS IN PROBLEM BEHAVIOR

If violent behavior is the destination, what path or paths lead to it? Loeber and Stouthamer-Loeber (1998a) point out that "few individuals begin a full-blown violent career. Instead, they 'ease' into it through minor offenses, and the earlier these begin, the more likely the individual will eventually show more serious examples of violent behavior." These researchers showed that the path to violence (e.g., rape, severe or lethal assault, and strong-arming) begins with what one could call minor aggression, such as bullying or annoying others.

For some, progression to physical fighting (fighting and gang fighting) follows. Relatively few children make the full journey to violence. Most boys who become violent have moved up through the whole pathway, rather than skipping steps. This finding is consistent with results reported by Elliott (1994) from the National Youth Survey that violence follows minor forms of aggression.

Another approach to problem behavior is found in the early-starter versus late-starter models of delinquent or antisocial behavior offered by Moffitt (1993). Violent behavior that has roots in early childhood aggression often persists and worsens in severity throughout childhood and into adulthood. It is suspected that many of the early-onset life-course boys would qualify for a diagnosis of attention-deficit/ hyperactivity disorder (ADHD) (Loeber & Stouthamer-Loeber, 1998a).

Patterson's work on a coercive parenting style based on escape-avoidance conditioning helps explain how an oppositional, disruptive, aggressive child may develop into a violent criminal. The ADHD child with oppositional behavior will challenge even the most committed and skillful parent. A parent with fewer resources for dealing with the challenge may respond with inconsistently coercive behavior. Initially, the parent is inclined to intervene with excessive force and negative affect—yelling, threatening, hitting, or grabbing to force compliance. This example becomes the child's blueprint for response to subsequent parental demands. Faced with the child's escalated defiance and aggression, the parent may withdraw or acquiesce. The child learns that obnoxious, coercive behavior pays off. It permits you to refuse an unwanted request or demand and get away without punishment.

This is a lesson that doesn't serve the child well in subsequent interactions outside the home. In addition to confrontational with authority figures such as teachers, the child who has been trained to use aggression to attain social goals faces rejection by peers. Aggressive children often respond to rejection and aggression from peers with an escalation of conflict. Still more rejection follows. As Fraser (1996) points out, the consequence of aggression is that the child becomes increasingly isolated from the social learning opportunities with prosocial peers. Neither parents nor peers offer the child a chance to learn negotiation, bargaining, cooperation, or willing acquiescence in the face of social conflict. Furthermore, these students' disruptive, confrontational stance toward the teacher and fellow students may put them at further risk for academic failure. Assignment to a special education class then increases association with similarly aggressive, socially rejected, and alienated children. They will bring out the worst in each other. From this cascade of negative effects will arise the deviant peer group of middle childhood, the precursor of the adolescent delinquent group or gang (Dishion, Patterson, Stoolmiller, & Skinner, 1991; Patterson, DeBaryshe, & Ramsey, 1989). Even after the early-starter male is no longer associated with the adolescent group, he is likely to continue to engage in violence and other forms of antisocial behavior (Loeber & Stouthamer-Loeber, 1998b).

Less stable is the violence and other misconduct associated with the late-starter path. Youth who do not begin their violence career until adolescence seem influenced less by family interaction patterns and more by school, peer, and neighborhood factors (Fraser, 1996). School practices that leave many adolescents feeling locked out of meaningful participation and that fail to offer opportunities to earn recognition for conventional activities invite these young people to look elsewhere for rewards. If association with deviant peers or participation in an illegitimate opportunity structure (e.g., drug dealing) beckons, the late-starter path may be entered. Those on the late-starter path often move away from violent offending as they settle down and move into adult roles in their twenties.

THE INTERTWINING OF DEVELOPMENTAL THREADS

Complex patterns of reciprocal causation *(vicious and virtuous circles)* and *cascading effects* can often be seen in the development of young people. One possibility is that the failure to acquire and exercise control of aggressive impulses leads to developmental failures and missteps in other realms. An example of this pattern has already been presented in the case of the oppositional child whose aggressive tendencies have been accentuated by parenting practices. Subsequently locking horns with teachers and peers alike, this child runs the risk of both academic failure and rejection by prosocial peers.

In the second case, failure at other developmental tasks, not directly involved with emotion and behavior regulation, eventually results in antisocial conduct. For example, a teenager's inability to keep up academically results in a loosening of the bond to the school and to the goal of academic achievement. Eventually the individual drops out and drifts toward others who are similarly detached from the school and from other venues of conventional, prosocial participation and achievement for which they have such inadequate preparation. A period of utilizing antisocial, possibly violent, means to achieve social and material goals follows.

In both of these examples, a failure to successfully perform age-related tasks is associated, although in different directions, with violence. This suggests an approach to violence prevention that will be discussed in greater detail later in this chapter—addressing those developmental failures that lead both to and from violence.

THE DEVELOPMENTAL SIGNIFICANCE OF EXPOSURE TO VIOLENCE

Direct victimization and co-victimization (witnessing violence) hurts children; that is clear. They are at least as likely to experience post-traumatic stress disorder (PTSD) symptoms in response to exposure as are adults, although certain PTSD symptoms (e.g., flashbacks and psychic numbing) are rarely seen in young children (Mazza & Overstreet, 2000; Osofsky & Osofsky, 2001). In preschool children, regressive features such as thumb sucking and loss of bowel and bladder control, sleep problems, crying, and insecure attachment to a caregiver are apparent (Guterman & Cameron, 1997).

School-age children may evidence psychic numbing and cognitive difficulties such as impaired memory or difficulty sustaining attention, as well as a reluctance to explore freely and master their environment (Osofsky, 1999). Exposure may lead some children to try to avoid situations that will trigger memories associated with the violent episode. Or the children may take the opposite route and focus on the experience, reenacting the event and perhaps fantasizing a last-minute rescue (Guterman & Cameron, 1997).

Anxiety and depressive symptoms—including guilt, lowered self-esteem, and worries about injuries—can be seen in school-age children, as can grief reactions if the community violence results in the injury or death of someone known by the children. On the other hand, frequent exposure to community violence can eventually lead to apparent habituation, with the child projecting an indifferent or nonchalant attitude toward violent events (Wallach, 1994).

Resignation, fatalism, and hopelessness appear in adolescents exposed to community violence. Given these assessments of the future, risk-taking behaviors may seem even more reasonable than is usually the case in adolescence (Guterman & Cameron, 1997). For other adolescents, feelings of vulnerability may prompt actions, such as carrying a weapon or joining a gang, that actually heighten risk (Kuther, 1999).

The developmental significance of exposure to violence extends beyond distress and the coping mechanisms employed to manage it. Children and adolescents need to involve and invest themselves in a number of important developmental tasks. This period of life is the one "in which individuals accumulate the various 'capitals,' human, social, and cultural, that shape the content of later lives" (Macmillan, 2001; Hagan, 2001).

If we ask how exposure to violence affects one of these human capitals, educational attainment, we can see a variety of mechanisms at play. One is the emotional turmoil described above (Kuther, 1999). Children who are experiencing PTSD symptoms, who are grieving, who are preoccupied with fears of injury—these children are in some sense beyond the reach of educational offerings directed at them (Bowen & Bowen, 1999; Lorion, 1998; Wallach, 1994). But it isn't just the children's emotional turmoil and its related distractions that can undermine education. Rather, the loss of control over life events that is involved in victimization compromises the person's sense of *agency* or *self-efficacy* (Kuther, 1999; Macmillan, 2001; Wallach, 1994). Without a sense of agency, it is pointless to set goals. Without a sense of self-efficacy, it makes no sense to expend effort or take risks to achieve these goals. Someone else can supply the goals and direct the effort in the short run. However, without a sense of self-efficacy (of being "up to the task"), the child is likely to overreact to minor failures and disappointments, perhaps abandoning all attempts to succeed at the task. Macmillan's (2001) study of adolescent victims of violence revealed that victimization led to a reduction of educational aspirations and effort, which subsequently resulted in lower occupational status in early adulthood.

Victimization and co-victimization might also threaten the child's trust in the social order and in other people. When violence can erupt at any moment, it is hard to feel at home and safe in a social setting. Willingness to engage in communal activities and to display guardianship of the setting may be lost.

In addition, the perception of others as potential predators may lead the child to shy away from them. This effectively destroys their value as social capital: the child cannot make use of their skills, advice, social connections, and so on, in pursuit of his or her own goals (Macmillan, 2001). Furthermore, an emphasis on the predatory threat from others might foster the kind of hostile attribution bias that leads a child to misinterpret innocent acts as aggressive and to react with hostility (Miller, Brehm, & Whitehouse, 1998; Tolan, Guerra, & Kendall, 1995). This kind of cognitive bias often leads to rejection by prosocial peers in childhood.

One final point regarding direct exposure to violence: victimization is a correlate of, perhaps a precursor to, perpetration of violent crime and involvement in other deviance (Lorion, 1998; Macmillan, 2001; Mazza & Overstreet, 2000; Williams & Stiffman, 1998). Multiple factors and mechanisms probably contribute to this robust finding. One possibility is that experience with victimization or co-victimization, especially repetitive experience, provides *social scripts* for the violent resolution of conflicts, as well as an apparent endorsement of the various motives and tactics employed (Guerra, Huesmann, Tolan, Acker, & Eron, 1995). Garbarino (Garbarino, Kostelny, & Dubrow, 1991b) has suggested that exposure to community violence truncates moral development and leads to a vendetta mentality that perpetuates a cycle of violence.

Another possibility involves a self-selection process, *niche picking*, which brings together individuals who are "looking for trouble." The individual gravitates toward violence-prone peers, either for protection from attack in an environment deemed threatening or merely because the violent behavior they display is compatible with his or her own preferred style. In either case, the concentration of persons who are quick to fight and slow to negotiate or compromise raises the risk that individual members will be caught up in a tinderbox of violence (Fagan & Wilkinson, 1998), both as victims and as perpetrators.

AN ECOLOGICAL-DEVELOPMENTAL APPROACH TO VIOLENCE IN YOUTH

As we have seen, aggression and violence both shape and are shaped by developmental trends. Bronfenbrenner's (1979) ecological-developmental model provides a way to structure existing youth violence research findings from multiple disciplines and to formulate a plan for further investigations, as well as prevention and intervention efforts. Its main elements are described by Williams et al. (1997):

- *Developmental stages* represent age grouping marked by changes in biology, social identity, and social settings, with five distinct stages spanning the period of infancy through adolescence.

- *Transitions* and *pathways* represent changes over the life course. *Transitions* refer to entry into new developmental stages, and *pathways* refer to the sequencing of transitions and experiences with stages over the life course.
- *Nested social contexts* refer to the multiple and interconnected contexts of development, including family, friends, school, community, and workplace.

As people move through these developmental stages, there is an endless interplay of (1) their personal characteristics (inherent or acquired) and (2) environmental supports or barriers to health-enhancing, developmentally appropriate outcomes. This person-in-context approach tracks movement through a progression of age-salient (though not age-limited) tasks and related environmental supports or barriers. The environmental supports or barriers change along with the tasks.

The developmental stage model includes these components:

- *developmental tasks*, which are demands for new forms of *competence*;
- *developmental needs*, which are the proximal resources that are repeatedly tapped to achieve success in specific developmental tasks;
- *developmental supports/barriers*, which are various supports or barriers to meeting developmental needs.

For example, progress in emotion and behavior regulation is a *developmental task* of infancy and toddlerhood. The related *developmental need* is a secure attachment to a caregiver (DeZulueta, 2001). *Developmental supports* are those resources that allow caregivers to be sensitive, warm, and contingently responsive to the infant's fluctuating states (i.e., to engage in behaviors that are likely to produce secure attachment). These supports include

- material resources that allow the caregiver and infant plenty of unhurried interaction;
- the caregiver's positive personality traits, positive and realistic expectations derived from attachment to his or her own caregiver, and skill at reading the infant's cues;
- affordable, high-quality day-care services that allow the child to develop stable attachments to caregivers outside the home.

We can, of course, gain additional understanding by looking for the barriers that impede the meeting of developmental needs. One that stands out for attachment is maternal depression, which affects infant emotional development even when physical care is adequate. We are then led to look for ways to ameliorate the mother's distress. These could include biological and cognitive treatment programs for the mother, as well as social and economic supports to alleviate or buffer specific stressors in her life.

Within this ecological-developmental framework, violence prevention is pursued by providing those environmental supports that yield

- developmental competence with regard to those hot-button challenges such as management of conflict, status-striving, self-protection, and regulating and expressing negative emotions;
- developmental competence with respect to tasks in other realms (e.g., academic achievement) so that failures here do not funnel children into deviant, antisocial associations and behavior patterns;
- ample opportunities and positive sanctions for using prosocial developmental competence.

That search for environmental supports (and the flip side, barriers) brings us to Bronfenbrenner's depiction of the environment, which is his most recognizable contribution. He imagines the environment as nested systems of interaction centered on the individual, who has characteristics that interact with environmental influences. The interplay between the individual and the environment is always, at least potentially, bidirectional. In the above example of coercive parenting, the child's preexisting ADHD and oppositional stance pull an exaggerated response from a poorly regulated parent. The child eventually responds to parental demands with a belligerence that mimics the parent's. Unable or unwilling to escalate the conflict, the parent sometimes backs off. This acquiescence, then, rewards the child's expression of hostility and resistance and increases the likelihood that it will be repeated. This example is consistent with Bronfenbrenner's view that the individual and environment are continually shaping each other.

Many of the child's most important environments are those that are close, in the sense that they envelope the child in frequent, face-to-face interaction. The individual seems to reside in these interactional environments, called *microsystems.*

But Bronfenbrenner's attention extends beyond the interactions between individuals within a microsystem. He wants us to consider the connections between microsystems, which he calls the *mesosystem.*

These may involve contacts between individuals representing each microsystem, but other kinds of connection are possible. The pattern of communication and the set of interactions between the school and the family is an example of this kind of environmental influence. In disadvantaged urban communities, these interactions between school and family are likely to be minimal, focused on problem behavior in school, and tainted with fear, resentment, and awkwardness (Astor et al., 1996). Parents do not inform the school of new stressors in the home that might help the teacher to understand disruptive behavior in the classroom. Teachers do not expect parents to monitor progress on homework assignments or to back up the teacher regarding classroom conduct. Mesosystem deficits such as these make it hard to fully support the development of the child in either microsystem.

Exosystems are systems in which the particular individual is not a direct participant. However, the interactions that take place and the decisions that are made in those exosystems may have far-reaching effects on the individual. Children do not sit on local school boards or citywide boards of education, but the decisions that emerge from them shape the everyday experiences of children in the classroom (Bowen & Bowen, 1999).

The *macrosystem* consists of the values, cultural understandings, priorities, shared history and symbols, and so forth that frame decision making and action within the other systems. Some aspects of the macrosystem are experienced rather directly. The culture of violence is brought right into our homes on a daily basis by various mass media, for example. But other macrosystem elements gain expression through the systems already mentioned, such as school boards. For example, within the U.S. macrosystem, commitment to universal education pairs with a commitment to local control and funding of education. The result has been enormous variations in both resources made available to schools and, ultimately, to the experiences of children in the microsystem of the classroom.

Bronfenbrenner's model is one of enormous scope, encouraging us to draw on findings from disciplines that use different levels of analysis and are preoccupied with different developmental issues. In the study of youth violence, psychology has focused on the individual's attributes, on early influences of the family and school microsystems. Sociology and criminology have provided an examination of adolescent development within the context of neighborhoods, communities, organizations, institutions, and their value systems.

Both of these contributions are visible in the early- versus late-starter model of antisocial behavior. For the early starter, individual neuropsychological characteristics and early socialization within the family and school are primary influences. But moving beyond these microsystems is especially important in the study of the adolescent late-starter criminal, who is thought to be influenced more by peer and neighborhood influences (Moffitt, 1993). Late starters appear in a variety of socioeconomic contexts. Indeed, Moffitt maintains that antisocial behavior in adolescence is so widespread during adolescence as to be normative; it is widespread because it is adaptive. But antisocial acts vary significantly in their form and their power to transform lives. Among African American young men, homicide is the leading cause of death, largely because antisocial acts so commonly involve the use of guns. Short of death, there are other *commitments* (e.g., police records) and *snares* (e.g., drug addiction) in antisocial behavior that may continue to haunt the individual long after adolescence has passed (Moffitt, 1993). Why don't adults—parents and community leaders—just put a stop to it?

Social disorganization theory (Laub & Lauritsen, 1998; Nash & Bowen, 1999; Sampson, 1997; Wandersman & Nation, 1998) provides an explanation of why it is so difficult for parents to keep their adolescent offspring out of trouble in inner-city disadvantaged neighborhoods. The argument is that as children move to adolescence, they spend more time away from the parents, with peers and with neighborhood associates. The control of the adolescent shifts from the home to the neighborhood or larger community. Certain features of an impoverished, inner-city neighborhood make it nearly impossible for a consensus to be reached regarding appropriate, prosocial behavior and for the monitoring and sanctioning of the adolescent's conduct with reference to this standard to occur. Neighborhoods marked by a great deal of residential turnover, poverty, ethnic and racial heterogeneity, single-parent families, and widespread unemployment leave people feeling isolated from neighbors and uncommitted to common values and practices. They are also isolated from mainstream economic opportunities in these neighborhoods where there are few legitimate jobs. Additionally, the inhabitants often lack the formal and informal social ties to the larger community outside the neighborhood that could be used to press for economic and social investment. Add to this an illegitimate opportunity structure (e.g., drug trafficking), and it becomes harder to keep young men and women from gravitating toward gangs or other peer groups that have an antisocial agenda (Hawkins, Farrington, & Catalano, 1998). To paraphrase an oft-quoted saying, "It takes a neighborhood to raise an adolescent." Bronfenbrenner's theory indicates that it takes a host of mesosystem, exosystem, and macrosystem supports to raise a neighborhood.

DEVELOPMENTAL STAGES AND PATHWAYS

Any developmental model that employs the notion of stages runs two risks: (1) movement between the stages will be conceived as being in lockstep, and (2) each stage will be seen as a fresh slate, a developmental challenge disconnected from the ones that go before and after it. Yet developmental models of competence must make it clear that success in a developmental task is at least partly contingent upon success in previous tasks, and that the current success contributes to readiness to master subsequent tasks. We bring our developmental baggage with us to each new stage. But the interdependence between stages is only partial. Past success doesn't guarantee current success; nor does past developmental difficulty always let loose a downward-rolling snowball of cumulative consequences. Although research on comprehensive early childhood family education programs makes it clear that getting off to a good start is helpful and even protects against delinquency (Greene, 1998; Masten & Coatsworth, 1998), it is also evident that there are *self-righting mechanisms* that help the person who has stumbled down a wrong path get back on track. It is this incomplete interdependence of developmental stages that makes us realize that individuals do not move in lockstep toward one end. Instead, we need to envision a variety of responses to developmental challenges that move people along different pathways, sometimes to different ends.

THE ECOLOGICAL-DEVELOPMENTAL
INTERPRETATION OF RESILIENCE

Currently, the concept of resilience enjoys high visibility, not just in the academic literature but also on the magazine stands of America (Doll & Lyon, 1998; Fitzpatrick, 1997; Fraser, Richman, & Galinsky, 1999; Gilgun, 1996; Grant, O'Koon, Davis, & Roache, 2000; Howard, Dryden, & Johnson, 1999; Jessor, 1993). The research pertaining to resilience explores one of the notions just mentioned: some people can beat the odds, so to speak, and achieve developmental competence *despite adversity, including developmental missteps.* A brief look at the concept of resilience will reveal a good deal of overlap with the ecological-developmental approach to competence.

The idea of resilience is a variation on the public health model that seeks to identify *risk* and *protective* factors related to well-being. Resilience is demonstrated when developmental competence is achieved *despite the presence of one or more risk factors for poor outcomes.* The person has been able to demonstrate competence in spite of the risk factors. Some risk factors are similar to what we have previously called *developmental barriers* in the ecological-developmental model; other risk factors could be attributes of the individual that impede the development of competence (e.g., low IQ). Protective factors are *developmental supports* or the *individual's attributes* that increase the prospects for healthy, competent outcomes (and reduce the chance of unhealthy or negative outcomes such as violence) despite risks. Some of the protective factors may be linked to the specific developmental tasks of a stage. Others have a usefulness that extends across more than one stage. And still others are remedial in the sense that they compensate for unmet needs in earlier periods (Williams et al., 1997).

In their review of the literature on the development of competence, Masten and Coatsworth (1998) identify a number of developmental tasks that they claim reflect both universal phenomena plus some more culturally specific tasks that are not universal. Table 1.1 lists age and developmental tasks widely agreed upon by developmental psychologists.

The authors then proceed to identify two systems of competence and one personal attribute that seem to be core or underlying in the sense that they are must-haves for a variety of developmental tasks. High IQ is the personal attribute, and it is interesting in that it seems not only to support good outcomes in general, but also to protect under conditions of vulnerability. Under duress, more intelligent children may show better problem solving, may be better able to attract the help of teachers, and may be better able to avoid behavior problems. Self-regulation is one of the systems of competence that underlies other achievements. For example, other competencies mentioned above, such as academic achievement, peer acceptance, and rule-governed conduct, would be impossible without self-regulation of emotions and behavior. The third core component is relationships with caring adults, and it also has adaptive significance across a variety

Table 1.1
Examples of Developmental Tasks

Age	Task
Infancy to preschool	Attachment to caregiver(s)
	Language
	Differentiation of self from environment
	Self-control and compliance
Middle childhood	School adjustment (attendance, appropriate conduct)
	Academic achievement (e.g., learning to read, do arithmetic)
	Getting along with peers (acceptance, making friends)
	Rule-governed conduct (following rules of society for moral behavior and prosocial conduct)
Adolescence	Successful transition to secondary schooling
	Academic achievement (learning skills needed for higher education or work)
	Involvement in extracurricular activities (e.g., athletics, clubs)
	Forming close friendships within and across gender
	Forming a cohesive sense of self: identity

Source: Masten and Coatsworth (1998).

of tasks (e.g., self-regulation, exploratory behavior, and smooth peer relations) (Carlson & Sroufe, 1995).

How does the child at risk—who suffers from a disability, poverty, or parental mental illness—manage to meet developmental tasks with some success? A review of the literature by Masten and Coatsworth (1998) resulted in a list of the qualities of the child and environment that are associated in many studies with good outcomes under adverse conditions. In Table 1.2, characteristics of resilient children and adolescents in the context of individual, family, and extrafamilial situations are listed. Descriptions of resilient children included in Table 1.2 are considered to be traits attained in normal development. These resilient children and adolescents have been described as obtaining important resources that provide emotional and psychosocial security (Masten & Coatsworth, 1998).

There is, as they point out, redundancy in the systems. If one adult—or even several adults—fail the child, there still exists the chance that someone else will step in to fill the void. The resilience literature is replete with examples of this substitution: a grandfather, teacher, pastor, or older sibling is credited by the resilient individual with serving a formative role in his or her development, usually by

Table 1.2
Characteristics of Resilient Children and Adolescents

Source	Characteristic
Individual	Good intellectual functioning
	Appealing, sociable, easygoing disposition
	Self-efficacy, self-confidence, high self-esteem
	Talents
	Faith
Family	Close relationships to caring parent figure
	Authoritative parenting: warmth, structure, high expectations
	Socioeconomic advantages
	Connections to extended supportive family networks
Extrafamilial	Bonds to prosocial adults outside the family
	Connections to prosocial organizations
	Attending effective schools

Source: Masten and Coatsworth (1998).

expressing high expectations for the child's future and then providing sustained involvement and guidance. This finding of the power of redundancy is a cause for optimism, especially for those who work with children with multiple risks and disadvantages. It suggests that there are multiple opportunities for getting it right, as it were, even when the child seems vulnerable.

Masten and Coatsworth sound a cautionary note about these findings. The adaptive value of some of the characteristics may depend on the situation (Stevenson, 1998). Although in general an easygoing, sociable disposition is protective (because it makes the child a very satisfying interaction partner for the caregiver and enhances the caregiver's sense of competence and motivation to assist the child), under some very adverse conditions, the child would be better off with a bad temper and a loud cry. During a drought in Africa, the difficult, irritable Masai babies had better survival rates, apparently another example of the squeaky wheel getting the oil (de Vries, 1984). Even the benefit of authoritative parenting, the highly touted benchmark for parental performance, may depend on the context. In contexts marked by high levels of danger, the child's immediate, unquestioning obedience to parental demands may be more protective than the give-and-take discussions that mark authoritarian parenting. Talking can wait; safety requires action that the parent must be empowered to choose. Similarly, conditions of substantial community violence may call for a higher level of parental monitoring of behavior than would be optimal in other settings.

What is most important to note here is that resilience is not a trait, not solely an attribute of the person. Rather, it is the outcome of an interaction between personal characteristics and environment supports in the face of developmental tasks made more difficult by risk factors. Of course, a history of negotiation of these developmental challenges may leave the person with many characteristics (e.g., skills, attitudes, and coping mechanisms) of proven success that are carried into new situations. But continued success will depend on the conditions confronted there (Gilgun, 1996).

THE ROLE OF THE SCHOOL IN VIOLENCE PREVENTION

What is the role of the school in violence prevention? According to the ecological-developmental perspective, it is the promotion of competence. It is clear that when it fails in this role and the child experiences academic failure, then the child is more likely to move in the direction of antisocial, perhaps violent, behavior (Hawkins et al., 1998). In addition to acquiring academic competence, the child must become attached to prosocial goals and standards of conduct, if the school is to succeed in preventing violence.

The major assumption of their *social development model* is that all behavior is learned through bonding with major social institutions (e.g., family, school, peer group). Bonding involves an attachment to others in the proximal social unit and a commitment to the actions, beliefs, and values endorsed by that unit. Once the bond is established, the child will usually act to preserve and strengthen the attachment and commitment. Hawkins and associates maintain that the development of bonds to schools is essential to ensure both academic achievement and the motivation to live according to the norms for nonviolent behavior. Children who manage to bond to the schools (i.e., who develop a commitment to learning and an attachment to the school community: to teachers and fellow students) will be more successful academically and will be less likely to engage in serious crime, including violent behavior (Hawkins et al., 1998; Kashani, Jones, Bumby, & Thomas, 1999).

Bonding is likely to occur when the school offers:

- *opportunities* for active involvement in the educational process (appropriate to the child's level of skills, in order to motivate engagement in learning);
- the development of *skills* or competencies (the exercise of which makes the opportunities for involvement satisfying);
- *sanctions* (reinforcement, rewards, recognition) for skillful involvement.

(This is referred to as the Skills-Opportunities-Sanctions, or S-O-S, model.)

In a review of the resilience literature, Benard (1995) makes many similar points regarding protective processes in schools. For the protective potential of the school to be realized, the children must experience there the same three categories of protective processes as they experience in a good home: caring relationships, high expectations combined with adequate support, and opportunities to contribute.

What does it take to build this kind of "sticky" bond? What must the school do to create the conditions for commitment and attachment?

- It has been suggested that the development of a *sense of caring relationships* may call for the following: creating one-on-one time with students; an appropriate amount of self-disclosure from the teacher; networking with family members, friends, and neighbors of students; using rituals and traditions to build a sense of community within the classroom; and providing emotional as well as academic support.
- Thematic, experiential, comprehensive curricula provide opportunities for *involvement,* as do programs that employ cooperative learning activities.
- Programs that allow students to be resources for each other build a sense of *involvement, achievement, and community.*
- *High expectations* can be expressed in a so-called mastery orientation, which stresses self-improvement, disciplined effort, and task mastery rather than competition.
- The progress of each student would need to be closely monitored and corrective instruction and tutoring provided to ensure that the designated *skills* were being acquired.

- The opportunity structure within the classroom and school must value a wide diversity of talents, skills, and learning styles; *recognition* should not be limited to a few top-ranked students in any endeavor.

The social development model seeks to build a *personal* relationship that fosters academic achievement through involvement and high standards, and it also seeks to build an emotional attachment that heightens the salience of a message of nonviolence. This message may be supported by specific conflict resolution programs, which supplement existing clear rules for conduct; and by consistent rule enforcement and the promotion of norms of nonviolence throughout the curriculum, classroom, and entire school. It is this entire package, the whole school context, that constitutes the prevention program.

STAGE MODELS OF COMPETENCE AND VIOLENCE PREVENTION

Samples and Aber (1998) take an approach to the question of violence prevention that is different, but still reflects the ecological-developmental orientation of building basic competence to reduce the appeal of violence. They consider four developmental stages, and for each one they identify the most critical developmental task that bears on violence prevention. They note that the features of the child's environment that are critically important for developmental success change with the tasks at each stage. These features are listed in Table 1.3.

After introducing the developmental task for each stage, Samples and Aber go on to speculate about some of the organizational or contextual variables that might affect success. For example, the development of self-regulation in early childhood is likely to depend on the quality of caretaking, which in turn might be influenced by caretaker/child ratios. In early adolescence, basic organizational features of the school that potentially impact the development of stable, prosocial peer groups include (1) the practice of changing classes with one's homeroom and (2) being instructed in a small environment, whether a classroom or a school-within-a-school. Social development during the transition from childhood to adolescence seems to be aided by the intimacy of a familylike setting in which the individual is readily recognized and can hope to actively participate.

Table 1.3
Building Competence

Stage/age	Developmental tasks
Early childhood (ages 2-5)	Development of self-regulation
Middle childhood (ages 6-11)	Development of normative beliefs about aggression; development of interpersonal negotiation strategies
Early adolescence (ages 12-14)	Development of stable, prosocial (vs. antisocial) peer group
Middle adolescence (ages 15-18)	Identity formation

Source: Samples and Aber (1998).

A review of violence prevention programs by age of targets is also presented by Samples and Aber (1998). They note that several long-term studies of early childhood programs that combine preschool programs and family support and education services have shown not only short-term improvements in self-regulation but also long-term reductions in antisocial behaviors, including those serious enough to warrant involvement in the criminal justice system (Yoshikawa, 1994). This robust, long-term impact on violent and nonviolent lawbreaking was a surprise in that it was not the primary goal of the prevention efforts. The goal of these programs was usually the promotion of intellectual and social competence among low-income children. The primary aim of the programs was to prepare disadvantaged young children for success in school. In addition to providing high-quality preschool programs, the experimental programs taught parenting skills and also helped parents to better understand their child's development so that they could support it more effectively. The finding that this multifaceted effort to build competence in the child and in the child's environment paid off in a variety of ways, including violence prevention, seems to validate the ecological-developmental position that it is through the promotion of competence that we prevent violence.

Programs for middle childhood are the now-familiar conflict management or resolution curricula that attempt to help children build skills for resolving conflict without resorting to violence. They typically employ three general approaches: (1) the teaching of cognitive, social, and emotional skills thought to aid in nonviolent conflict management (e.g., active listening, perspective taking, negotiation, anger management), (2) the promotion of prosocial attitudes and values, and (3) instruction in the risk factors or triggers that can lead to violence (Greene, 1998). Although widely adopted by school systems throughout the country, these curricula have not been adequately researched to allow them to be judged effective.

As Samples and Aber move on to the consideration of early and middle adolescence, their review of studies reveals a curious disconnect between the stated developmental tasks and the age-related programs. Most of the programs chosen for review continue to focus narrowly on attitudes toward violence, conflict resolution, anger management, and communication skills. Although there is no doubt that many adolescents need such instruction, the adolescent tasks involving peers and identity are largely ignored.

Moffitt's taxonomy of adolescent-limited and life-course-persistent antisocial behavior provides an answer to these questions. The life-course-persistent pattern begins with a neuropsychological deficit, often fairly subtle, that may be expressed in temperament (e.g., emotional reactivity, irritability), behavioral development (e.g., problems with speech, language learning, impulse control), and cognitive development (e.g., problems with attention, language, memory, and reasoning). At risk of being clumsy, inattentive, impulsive, irritable, overactive, or deficient in verbal comprehension and expression (Johnson, 1996), children with these inborn neuropsychological disadvantages may not be born to able parents who can address these special needs (Moffitt, 1993). Instead, they are raised by parents who tend to resemble them in personality and in cognitive ability. A pattern of disruptive interaction subsequently spreads to the school and then to the larger community. Persistent and frequent offending by these individuals is accompanied by other antisocial behaviors, such as drug and alcohol abuse; multiple and unstable relationships; child abuse, neglect, or abandonment; homelessness; spousal abuse; and psychiatric illness (Fraser, 1996; Moffitt, 1993).

A much different picture emerges for adolescent-limited misconduct. It doesn't reflect individual deviance so much as a response to a dilemma shared by age-mates. A secular change in both the age of onset of puberty and the age at entry into employment and other adult roles has lengthened adolescence as a period of transition from childhood to adulthood. The coincidence of earlier puberty and later entry into adult roles has led some researchers to comment on young people's isolation into a type of age ghetto that prevents the biological and social ages from convening (Moffitt, 1993). Biologically ready for adulthood but denied access to its benefits, they remain dependent on, and controlled by, their families and discounted by much of society. As they make the transition into high school, these youths encounter older males, often life-course-persistent antisocial individuals, who have elaborated a delinquent lifestyle that grants them the prerequisites of adulthood: intimate relationships with the opposite sex, consumption of drugs and alcohol, material goods (especially cars and clothes), and so on. And they are stunningly unencumbered by family interference in their lives. The newcomers observe the antisocial means by which these benefits were obtained, and then set out to mimic them.

Provoking responses from adults in authority, finding ways to look older, tempting fate, damaging rapport with parents—all are suspected symbolic reinforcements added to the material and sensual benefits obtained by the antisocial behavior. So why do youth ever give it up? First, they emerge from the maturity gap to assume real adult roles. There is no need to try to *appear* to be an adult when you are already recognized as one.

Further, the legitimate benefits currently flowing from these adult roles may well be compromised by antisocial behavior; the young adult has a stake in the social order now. Of course, some adults will find it difficult to leave a deviant lifestyle because of the damaging consequences of their adolescent flirtation with antisocial conduct. Moffitt believes that these *snares* (e.g., teenage pregnancy, a criminal record) will slow down, but not necessarily stop, the movement away from delinquency.

Moffitt sees delinquent behavior as essentially adaptive and responsive to changes in contingencies: the deviant route to mature status with all its privileges will be abandoned when the conventional route becomes available. A similar view is put forth by Fagan and Wilkinson (1998) regarding the functions of adolescent violence in disadvantaged, inner-city neighborhoods. Like teens in other communities, those in disadvantaged neighborhoods are experiencing an array of physical, emotional, and social transformations. They are moving into new, more complex and competitive social environments as they advance to middle school and then high school. Expectations held by others for them are changing, as are their own expectations for themselves. Their behavior is guided by what Fagan and Wilkinson (1998) have described as the universal goals of adolescence: to achieve social affiliation, mastery, social identity, and autonomy. But like the adolescent that Moffitt described (1993), the inner city teen is frustrated in the pursuit of his or her goals.

Within the context of the inner city, violence serves several functions important to adolescents, according to Moffitt (1993); they are as follows:

- *Impression management: achieving and maintaining high status.* Displays of male toughness give pleasure, gain status, evidence street style, and deter attacks.

- *Materialism, status, and social identity.* Material wealth leads to status. Carefully chosen, so-called props are part of a sorting process that occurs during adolescence; their expense may prompt theft. Pleasure may be obtained by taking possessions from another.

- *Power.* Violence may be used to dominate, and possibly humiliate, opponents.

- *Rough justice, social control, and self-help.* Street culture demands retribution for lack of "respect." (See also Baumeister et al., 1996.) Violence is used to regulate illegal activities such as drug dealing. Preemptive violence has deterrent value.

- *Defiance of authority.* An "oppositional culture" expresses a sense of unfairness of the social order. Pursuit of conventional success is rejected as a betrayal of others in the community.

From an ecological-development viewpoint that stresses competence promotion as a mechanism for violence prevention, it would seem important to provide alternative methods of achieving competence in adolescent developmental tasks (e.g., affiliation, identity, autonomy, mastery)—methods that do not partake of violence (Corvo, 1997). After-school and weekend activities sponsored by the schools or other organizations potentially provide what could be termed an urban sanctuary, where violence is escaped while a variety of developmental needs are addressed.

For example, if identify formation is a developmental task targeted by a program, then participants might be offered a chance to venture beyond the familiar in an exploration of occupational roles, with the program serving as a bridge to internships, summer jobs, and volunteer activities, including those outside the immediate neighborhood. Mentors and other contact persons could be introduced and connected to the group as a whole or to individuals within it. These occupational guides could clarify the way that their everyday occupational activities draw on their educational preparation and help adolescents better grasp the pathways through the educational system. Whereas adolescents from a variety of contexts, including the most affluent, suffer from isolation from the workplace, youth in inner-city neighborhoods may be especially disadvantaged in this regard because of the scarcity of legitimate jobs within the neighborhood and lack of ties between the neighborhood and the larger community. Additional effort to expand horizons is needed if the youth are to envision a future that calls them away from the illegitimate opportunity structure within their community.

Good programs can address multiple developmental goals (e.g., identity, affiliation, mastery, and autonomy) simultaneously. To be effective as developmental supports and not just as shelters from violence (Halpern, Barker, & Mollard, 2000), programs for adolescents probably need to promote the kind of sticky bond that was discussed with regard to effective schools. To that end, they will offer the following:

- challenges and activities that are real, in the sense of being consequential and valued by their communities, rather than manufactured to entertain, occupy, or contain the adolescents (McLaughlin & Irby, 1994);
- opportunities to develop and demonstrate status-conferring skills and accomplishments, tests of physical endurance and power being especially important for inner-city males (Chaiken, 1998);
- a group identity and organization traditions (Chaiken, 1998);
- opportunities to exercise some autonomy, within the context of organization rules that are clear;
- familylike environments in which individuals are valued (McLaughlin & Irby, 1994);
- adults that communicate caring, personal interest, and commitment.

This is reminiscent of the S-O-S model advocated by Williams et al. (1997) as a foundation for programming based on providing developmental supports for (or reducing developmental barriers to) developmental needs as a method of violence prevention. Further description and analysis of good programs can be found in chapter 5 ("The

Teaching of Violence Prevention in a School Setting—What Can Be Done?," by Pichler, Urban, and Bockewitz) and chapter 9 ("Research Issues Related to Conflict Resolution Intervention Programs," by Sexton-Radek).

CONCLUSION

Bronfenbrenner's ecological-developmental model has been used here to frame the consideration of violence and its prevention. Although allowing for the possibility that violent behavior can be adaptive under various ecological conditions, we see it generally as a manifestation of developmental incompetence, a failure to master age-salient developmental tasks. From this viewpoint, where violence is common, there is likely to be an ecological failure to provide developmental support for competence. Additional specification of these tasks and their supports should allow us to better identify when and how development is going off course. A plan for corrective action requires that we understand the microsystem, mesosystem, exosystem, and macrosystem contributions to the ecological failure, as well as their potential contribution to developmental supports.

REFERENCES

Astor, R.A., Pitner, R.I., & Duncan, B.B. (1996). Ecological approaches to mental health consultation with teachers on issues related to youth and school violence. *Journal of Negro Education, 65,* 336–355.

Baumeister, R.F., Smart, L., & Boden, J.M. (1996). Relation of threatened egotism to violence and aggression: The dark side of high self-esteem. *Psychological Review, 103,* 5–33.

Benard, B. (1995). Fostering resilience in children. *ERIC Digest* (EDO-PS-95–99).

Bowen, N.K., & Bowen, G.L. (1999). Effects of crime and violence in neighborhoods and schools on the school behavior and performance of adolescents. *Journal of Adolescent Research, 14,* 319–342.

Bronfenbrenner, U. (1979). *The ecology of human development.* Cambridge, MA: Harvard University Press.

Chaiken, M. (1998). Tailoring established after-school programs to meet urban realities. In D.S. Elliott, B.A. Hamburg, & K.R. Williams (Eds.), *Violence in American schools: A new perspective* (pp. 348–375). New York: Cambridge University Press.

Corvo, K. N. (1997). Community-based youth violence prevention: A framework for planners and funders. *Youth and Society, 28,* 291–316.

de Vries, M. (1984). Temperament and infant mortality among the Masai of East Africa. *American Journal of Psychiatry, 141,* 1189–1194.

DeZulueta, F. (2001). Understanding the evolution of psychopathology and violence. *Criminal Behaviour and Mental Health, 11,* 17–22.

Dishion, T. J., Patterson, G. R., Stoolmiller, M., & Skinner, M. L. (1991). Family, school, and behavioral antecedents to early adolescent involvement with antisocial peers. *Developmental Psychology, 27,* 172–180.

Doll, B., & Lyon, M. A. (1998). Risk and resilience: Implications for the delivery of educational and mental health services in schools. *School Psychology Review, 27,* 348–362.

Elliott, D. S., Hamburg, B., & Williams, K. R. (1998). Violence in American schools: An overview. In D. S. Elliott, B. A. Hamburg, & K. R. Williams (Eds.), *Violence in American schools: A new perspective* (pp. 3–28). New York: Cambridge University Press.

Fagan, J., & Wilkinson, D. L. (1998). Social contexts and functions of adolescent violence. In D. S. Elliott, B. A. Hamburg, & K. R. Williams (Eds.), *Violence in American schools: A new perspective* (pp. 55–93). New York: Cambridge University Press.

Fitzpatrick, K. (1997). Fighting among America's youth: A risk and protective factors approach. *Journal of Health and Social Behavior, 38,* 131–148.

Fraser, M. W. (1996). Aggressive behavior in childhood and early adolescence: An ecological-developmental perspective on youth violence. *Social Work, 41,* 347–361.

Fraser, M. W., Richman, J. M., & Galinsky, M. J. (1999). Risk, protection, and resilience: Toward a conceptual framework for social work practice. *Social Work Research, 23,* 131–143.

Garbarino, J., Kostelny, K., & Dubrow, N. (1991a). What children can tell us about living in danger [1989 APA Award recipient address presented at 1990 convention]. *American Psychologist, 46,* 376–383.

Garbarino, J., Kostelny, K., & Dubrow, N. (1991b). *No place to be a child: Growing up in a war zone.* Lexington, MA: Lexington Books.

Gilgun, J. F. (1996). Human development and adversity in ecological perspective, part 1: A conceptual framework. *Families in Society, 77,* 395–402.

Grant, K., O'Koon, J., Davis, T., & Roache, N. (2000). Protective factors affecting low-income urban African Americans exposed to stress. *Journal of Early Adolescence, 20,* 388–417.

Greene, M. B. (1998). Youth violence in the city: The role of educational interventions. *Health Education and Behavior, 25,* 175–193.

Guerra, N. G., Huesmann, L. R., Tolan, P. H., Acker, R. V., & Eron, L. D. (1995). Stressful events and individual beliefs as correlates of economic disadvantage and aggression among urban children [Special section: Prediction and prevention of child and adolescent antisocial behavior]. *Journal of Consulting and Clinical Psychology, 63,* 518–528.

Guterman, N., & Cameron, M. (1997). Assessing the impact of community violence on children and youths. *Social Work, 42,* 495–505.

Hagan, J. (2001). Youth violence and the end of adolescence. *American Sociological Review, 6,* 874–899.

Halpern, R., Barker, G., & Mollard, W. (2000). Youth programs as alternative spaces to be: A study of neighborhood youth programs in Chicago's West town. *Youth and Society, 31,* 469–506.

Harris and Associates, Inc. (1996). *The Metropolitan Life survey of the American teacher 1996: Students voice their opinions on violence, social tension, and equality among teens.* New York: Author.

Hawkins, J. D., Farrington, D. P., & Catalano, R. F. (1998). Reducing violence through the schools. In D. S. Elliott, B. A. Hamburg, & K. R. Williams (Eds.), *Violence in American schools: A new perspective* (pp. 188–216). New York: Cambridge University Press.

Howard, S., Dryden, J., & Johnson, B. (1999). Childhood resilience: Review and critique of literature. *Oxford Review of Education, 25,* 307–323.

Jessor, R. (1993). Successful adolescent development among youth in high-risk settings. *American Psychologist, 48,* 117–126.

Johnson, H. C. (1996). Violence and biology: A review of the literature. *Families in Society, 77,* 3–18.

Kashani, J. H., Jones, M. R., Bumby, K. M., & Thomas, L. A. (1999). Youth violence: Psychosocial risk factors, treatment, prevention, and recommendations. *Journal of Emotional and Behavioral Disorders, 7,* 200–210.

Kuther, T. L. (1999). A developmental-contextual perspective on youth co-victimization by community violence. *Adolescence, 136,* 699–714.

Laub, J. H., & Lauritsen, J. L. (1998). The interdependence of school violence with neighborhood and family conditions. In D. S. Elliott, B. A. Hamburg, & K. R. Williams (Eds.), *Violence in American schools: A new perspective* (pp. 127–155). New York: Cambridge University Press.

Loeber, R., & Hay, D. (1997). Key issues in the development of aggression and violence from childhood to early adulthood. *Annual Review of Psychology, 48,* 371–410.

Loeber, R., & Stouthamer-Loeber, M. (1998a). Development of juvenile aggression and violence: Some common misconceptions and controversies [Special issue: Applications of developmental science]. *American Psychologist, 53,* 242–259.

Loeber, R., & Stouthamer-Loeber, M. (1998b). Juvenile aggression at home and at school. In D. S. Elliott, B. A. Hamburg, & K. R. Williams

(Eds.), *Violence in American schools: A new perspective* (pp. 94–126). New York: Cambridge University Press.

Lorion, R. (1998). Exposure to urban violence: Contamination of the school environment. In D.S. Elliott, B.A. Hamburg, & K.R. Williams (Eds.), *Violence in American schools: A new perspective* (pp. 293–311). New York: Cambridge University Press.

Macmillan, R. (2001). Violence and the life course: The consequences of victimization for personal and social development. *Annual Review of Sociology, 27,* 1–22.

Masten, A., & Coatsworth, J. (1998). The development of competence in favorable and unfavorable environments: Lessons from research on successful children [Special issue: Applications for developmental science]. *American Psychologist, 53,* 205–220.

Mazza, J.J., & Overstreet, S. (2000). Children and adolescents exposed to community violence: A mental health perspective for school psychologists. *School Psychology Review, 29,* 86–101.

McLaughlin, M.W., & Irby, M.A. (1994). Neighborhood organizations that keep hope alive. *Phi Delta Kappan, 76,* 300–306.

Miller, G.E., Brehm, K., & Whitehouse, S. (1998). Reconceptualizing school-based prevention for antisocial behavior within a resiliency framework. *School Psychology Review, 27,* 364–379.

Moffitt, T. (1993). Adolescence-limited and life-course-persistent antisocial behavior: A developmental taxonomy. *Psychological Review, 100,* 674–701.

Nash, J.K., & Bowen, G.L. (1999). Perceived crime and informal social control in the neighborhood as a context for adolescent behavior: A risk and resilience perspective. *Social Work Research, 23,* 171–186.

Osofsky, J.D. (1999). The impact of violence on children. *The Future of Children, 9,* 33–37.

Osofsky, H.J., & Osofsky, J.D. (2001). Violent and aggressive behaviors in youth: A mental health and prevention perspective. *Psychiatry, 64,* 285–295.

Patterson, G.R., DeBaryshe, B.D., & Ramsey, E. (1989). A developmental perspective on antisocial behavior. *American Psychologist, 44,* 329–335.

Reppucci, N.D., Wollard, J.L., & Fried, C.S. (1999). Social, community, and preventive interventions. *Annual Review of Psychology, 50,* 387–418.

Samples, F., & Aber, L. (1998). Evaluations of school-based violence prevention programs. In D.S. Elliott, B.A. Hamburg, & K.R. Williams (Eds.), *Violence in American schools: A new perspective* (pp. 217–252). New York: Cambridge University Press.

Sampson, R.J. (1997). Collective regulation of adolescent misbehavior: Validation results from eighty Chicago neighborhoods. *Journal of Adolescent Research, 12,* 227–244.

Stevenson, H. (1998). Raising safe villages: Cultural-ecological factors that influence the emotional adjustment of adolescents. *Journal of Black Psychology, 24,* 44–59.

Tolan, P.H., Guerra, N.G., & Kendall, P.C. (1995). A developmental-ecological perspective on antisocial behavior in children and adolescents: Toward a unified risk and intervention framework. *Journal of Consulting and Clinical Psychology, 63,* 579–584.

Wallach, L.B. (1994). Violence and young children's development. *ERIC Digest* (ED369578).

Wandersman, A., & Nation, M. (1998). Urban neighborhoods and mental health: Psychological contributions to understanding toxicity, resilience, and interventions [Special issue: Psychology in the public forum]. *American Psychologist, 53,* 647–656.

Williams, J., & Stiffman, A. (1998). Violence among urban African American youths: An analysis of environmental and behavioral risk factors. *Social Work Research, 22,* 3–13.

Williams, K.R., Guerra, N.G., & Elliott, D.S. (1997). *Human development and violence prevention: A focus on youth* (Center for the Study and Prevention of Violence Paper 011). Boulder, CO: Center for the Study and Prevention of Violence, University of Colorado at Boulder.

Yoshikawa, H. (1994). Prevention as cumulative prevention: Effects of early family support and education on chronic delinquency and its risks. *Psychological Bulletin, 115,* 28–54.

Chapter 2

PSYCHOANALYTIC/ DEVELOPMENTAL THEORIES RELATED TO ADOLESCENCE AND AGGRESSION

Charles E. Goldsmith

This chapter follows in the footsteps of Peter Blos when in his study of adolescence he remarked: "It is an attempt, above all else, to reflect basic concepts which I have abstracted from my clinical work and which, over time, have been conditioned by way of observing human behavior and contemplating its nature and development"(Blos, 1979, p. 3).

DEFINITIONS

A traditional definition of *aggression* is reflected by Baron and Richardson (1994) in his distinction between aggression and dominance. Baron proposed that aggression be considered an overt behavior that has the intention to cause harm to someone. Moyer (1968) expanded this type of definition to include the component of a goal being blocked intentionally. Such a restrictive definition of aggression does not include assertive and intrusive behaviors, which are generally not destructive. Both the research and the treatment of human assertive, aggressive, hostile, and violent behaviors have been hampered by a highly variable but poorly developed nosology.

According to *Diagnostic and Statistical Manual of Mental Disorders* (American Psychiatric Association, 2000; DSM-IV) mental disorder criteria, violent behavior in an adolescent might generate a Conduct Disorder diagnosis (Conduct Disorder, Under-socialized, Aggressive;

or Conduct Disorder, Socialized, Aggressive). In an adult such behavior might be categorized as either an Isolated or Intermittent Explosive Disorder, or such behavior might not be classified as a mental disorder at all. For example, in certain cases of child abuse, the behavior might be categorized as a DSM-IV "V Code" of Parent-Child Problem. Hostile or violent behavior might also be considered a symptom of other psychological or psychiatric disorders, including dementia, schizophrenia, alcohol or other drug intoxication, depression, mania, antisocial personality disorder, mental retardation, or attention-deficit disorder.

A review of the literature and observations in the clinical setting over a period of 30 years indicates that aggression does not always have as its objective the intention of inflicting damage. The working definition I have used in the clinical setting has followed a model extracted from a developmental approach.

THEORIES OF AGGRESSIVE BEHAVIOR

Several theories have attempted to explain human aggressive behavior. These reflect in part the persistent nature-nurture conflicts that have permeated psychology. Freud hypothesized an aggressive drive state—Thanatos—that was directed toward death and destruction (Freud, 1930). The drive theory of aggression was popularized by Konrad Lorenz's book *Studies in Animal and Human Behavior*, in which Lorenz described a drive state in humans that builds up aggressive urges that eventually "spill over" and are released (Lorenz, 1970). Intervention in such a theoretical system requires a rechanneling of the release of these urges in less destructive ways.

The frustration-aggression theory proposed by Dollard and associates in the 1930s also conceptualized a type of reservoir of aggressive energy seeking an outlet (Dollard et al., 1939). According to this theory, the interruption of goal-directed behavior by the external environment increases the probability of aggressive behavior. If the interrupted behavior is highly motivated, the probability of aggression is greater than in low-motivation situations. If the goal-directed behavior is repeatedly blocked, the probability of destructive aggression increases proportionally with the "frustration."

In contrast to the drive theories of aggression are the social learning theories (Anderson, 1997). Within this theoretical system, organisms learn hostile and violent behavior through modeling or random activity. Violence is sustained by positive reinforcement contingencies. Moreover, the cognitive paradigms of the learning theory can be utilized to disinhibit, so to speak, aggressive behavior by overcoming either innate or early learned inhibitions toward violence through the use of such techniques as desensitization or dehumanization of the victim.

The biological and psychiatric treatment model of human aggression disorders fits most easily into the conceptualization of aggression as a drive state seeking expression. Interventions (i.e., medications) can affect the development of the drive; for example, by decreasing frustration or the organism's perception of frustration. This can also block the discharge of the drive or render the discharge less impulsive. Upon this biological matrix, learning theory can also be applied. Contemporary clinical intervention most often utilizes both approaches (Lieberman & Greenberg, in press).

A DEVELOPMENTAL MODEL

Another approach to a study of aggression, and especially aggression in adolescents, is a developmental model. Here we are looking at a broader context that includes age-related changes but also shifts that occur in the developmental mechanisms of object relations.

Anger, the first aggressive expression, appears to be an inborn affect and, like the other affects, is a capacity that exists from birth and that is evoked by environmental triggers (Tomkins, 1978). In the most in-depth and widely cited study of the development of aggression in childhood, Henri Parens (1979) concluded that aggression is inborn but inherently nondestructive. Ascribing the importance of aggression to motivating play and exploration, Parens found that its purpose is mastery of the environment. This view was confirmed by Plaut in his paper "Play and Adaptation" (1979). Rather than an inherently destructive drive in any form, aggression appears to be an adaptive response of the emerging self, important to both the growth of the self and its protection and security. In the normal situation, as aggression is employed to these ends, it serves the purpose of self-realization.

Parens found that there is a clear distinction among forms of aggression. Spontaneous, inborn aggression is not hostile and possesses no destructive intent but serves the adaptive purpose of exploration and learning about and controlling the environment. If all goes well, this form of aggression, which first appears in almost all infants between 8 and 16 weeks, eventually leads to self-assertiveness.

When, inevitably, the environment resists a child's unfettered exploration and assertiveness, with the mother or later with peer conflict, or there is excessive delay in achieving a goal, a child experiences displeasure, which then may lead to an overlay of hostile or possible violent aggression. Parens found that this form of aggression is a reaction to negative experience, most typically threat and endangerment. When the source of displeasure is removed, the hostile aggression stops. For example, if a toddler is busy at play, and a rival child reaches for his or her toy, the child may respond aggressively to the intruder, intending to cause him or her to back off. If the response is successful, the hostile aggression, having achieved its purpose, abates, thereby allowing the child to resume play, continuing the imaginative exploration and discovery of the world that is needed for enrichment and growth.

If, on the other hand, negative experience is not typically removed by environmental provision, and it becomes repetitive, the hostile aggression may grow into an automatic and chronic pattern, or complex, which is an overlay and so-called at hand, but not necessarily a part of the emerging self. In this situation, aggression, no longer serving the purpose of learning and mastery, becomes deflected to the continual discharge of hostility or escalated to violence. The residual is hatred (Akhtar, 1996).

Now imbued with an overlay of a destructive intent of hostility and violence, aggression may be excessively prohibited, as by repression, splitting, or denial, and a critical resource for normal object relations of self-development. The phases of *systemic, narcissistic, amoric, erotic,* and *altruistic* dynamics will be limited or lost developmentally, and thus may impair the child's ability to realize his or her self-potential.

These object relations of developmental dynamics found in childhood repeat themselves in an extended environment of object relations in adolescence through a type of recapitulation, as it were, of the systemic, narcissistic, amoric, erotic, and altruistic phases or mechanisms of development. In adolescence even more poignantly, when the defense fails, the overlay of aggression on the relation between self and object, when it is activated as a psychic complex, tends to burst forth in a seemingly uncontrolled, disorganized fashion. Just as in early childhood, so in early adolescence, outbursts of rage may then appear to be impulses, but as has been proposed here, such eruptions are an overlay, a product of repression or other defenses against aggression rather than a breaking through of drive impulses that have failed to be sufficiently repressed. Under these circumstances, aggression looks like a drive with inherent hostile intent, but, in fact, the hostility is a transformation of the original nondestructive aggression both in childhood and later in adolescence. Furthermore, if there is excessive delay in the expression of hostile destructiveness, its eventual discharge may be experienced as relieving, resulting in the pleasurable destructiveness of teasing, taunting, and sadism in childhood, and in bullying, rowdiness, and roughness in adolescence, and, at a more excessive level, in violent destructiveness.

Parens's (1979) results indicated that children whose distress was not well responded to felt helpless, with no way to relieve the source of pain (compare Spitz, 1965). This type of helplessness is also experienced in adolescence with boredom, with no way to relieve the ennui (Eissler, 1978). For these individuals, whether children or adolescents, hostility (aggressiveness in the form of destruction) distances them from their assertive/creative self and from others, which had protected them from repeated painful, helpless experiences. As viewed in the clinical setting, the chronic, automatic hostility (complex) of these children served the critical function of protecting the vulnerability of the self, but kept them from the normal dynamics of object relations. This deflection of aggression from its purpose of self-assertion and creativity to the defense of the vulnerable self defines pathological aggression and is precisely the function of hostility described by Kohut (1977). Parens concluded that the automaticity (what we have referred to here as a second layering of the self) of hostile aggression and the gratification it provides are not inborn but a function of unresponsive object relations and bear the history of these relationships.

The assumption that aggression is inherently destructive is made not only by drive-based theorists such as Freud, the Kleinians, and Kernberg but also by such nondrive authors as Winnicott, Fairbairn, and even Mitchell (see Berkowitz, 1993, for more information about these theories). All of these theoreticians equate the hostile intent of pathological aggression with normal aggression, failing to distinguish the infant's natural, and later the early adolescent's, joy in aggression, from an overlay on the self–object relation in the form of hatred. Parens's findings support Kohut's concept that assertiveness is inborn, but hatred (hostility and violence) is a pathological breakdown in response mechanisms to threats to the self both in infancy, and, as we have extended these dynamics, into adolescence.

Thus, aggression may be seen as prototypical of inborn capacities, and from the point of view of this chapter, also of the so-called new world of adolescence. Although it has a natural trajectory, that is, through the object-relations dynamics of the systemic, narcissistic, amoric, erotic, and altruistic phases, aggression requires an object to achieve its purpose and a developmental mechanism to carry it. If derailed by unfavorable responsiveness, aggression becomes deflected from its original goal of environmental exploration and mastery to serve other, self-protective aims in childhood and again in adolescence. We label these deflected purposes an overlay on the self–object relation and pathological precisely because they no longer serve their original purpose, although they leave signs of this deflection in the form of symptoms.

COMPONENTS OF A DEVELOPMENTAL MODEL

The components of a developmental model of aggressiveness in adolescence, as in childhood, include *assertive behavior, aggressive behavior, hostile behavior,* and *violent behavior.*

Assertive behavior focuses on maintaining recognition, an averment or declaration, not necessarily supported by a hostile or violent aim. Following the principle of orthogenesis, proposed by Werner (1948), development is a process of increasing differentiation and specification of the organism's relatively global organization and a hierarchic integration of the more individuated systems so that progressive equilibrium is achieved. Structurally, more primitive systems have no definite boundaries but are diffuse in both internal character and external relationship to each other, and thus, in our discussion, leave the early experience of self open to assault. Assertiveness then, represents a more primitive behavior of determination on a spectrum that moves toward identifying the aim and the object of energy displacement.

Aggression is more hierarchically organized than assertiveness in object relations, and its focus is more specific. At the assertive level children may hit with no other objective than the release of energy. In adolescence assertiveness shows itself as it had in childhood but now with a more extended frame of reference, in exploration and discovery. As a child becomes more aggressive, an aim and object may be differentiated. The aim may be the release of frustration or a reaction to boredom, which is often identified as acting-out behavior, or, with the purpose of affecting an object, may be termed out-of-bounds behavior. When we look at adolescence these two types can to be further recognized and differentiated.

As has been identified, neither assertive nor aggressive behaviors have an intrinsic, destructive component. In working with adolescents it is important to distinguish behavior that is assertive and aggressive, which is not intended to inflict damage, from hostile and violent behaviors, which have the aim of damage or destruction.

Thus, in the clinical setting, it is important to recognize that assertive and aggressive behaviors may move toward creativity, or toward agonistic behaviors of hostility and violence. Actions surrounding mating, for example, have both assertive and aggressive behaviors but are not necessarily destructive. Jan Jewett's (1992) paper on aggression and cooperation describes strategic approaches by which children can manage themselves around or with other children.

Hostility focuses on the damaging or destructive element with a specific aim and object in mind. Furthermore, violence may have the aim of destruction without necessarily being limited to a specific object. In violence the fury, intensity, and severity may overreach the object and spill out into indiscriminate destruction.

ADOLESCENCE

Usually, adolescence is marked by the onset of puberty, with a sociological ending of adult status. The sex drive becomes pronounced after a relative latency, depending on the society, and sexual and growth changes are accompanied by an increase in energy and emotional tumult, again, depending on the society. It is these latter phenomena that have the most direct effect on the family and are most directly affected by cultural role prescriptions and family behavior in generativity (McAdams, Hart, & Maruna, 1998).

In some nonliterate and preindustrial societies rites of passage symbolized the attainment of adult status. The individual usually engaged in his or her adult occupational activities from early childhood. Marriage represented a final attainment of full adult status. In industrial and technological societies, adolescence, as a status with a disparate biological and social termination, often becomes protracted and defined as a social problem. Developments in science and technology make necessary an increasingly lengthened period of formal training for young people. The increased energy characteristic of this biological stage of the life cycle is, furthermore, not usually channeled into productive work until after, and sometimes long after, the attainment of puberty.

The marginal status that adolescence represents is extended at both ends. It not only ends later; it begins earlier. The interim period between childhood and socially recognized adulthood is not a time of unrestrained freedom. Behavior is regulated, and often very stringently, especially by peer groups. Collective behavior "proneness to fads, fashions, and social movements" is characteristic of individuals who occupy an insecure or marginal status. Since they are not locked into established patterns, they are more available to what is new and different.

Adolescence is not a paradise of nonresponsibility, as it has often been depicted. In mobile, class societies it is a time of uncertainty, especially in preparation and competition for jobs and marital partners. The family can guarantee neither in an industrial and technological society, although it plays a role in limiting possible choices. In traditional societies, the family not only limited but often determined both the occupation and the mate. The adolescent did not have to ask: "Who am I?" or "What will I be when I grow up?" The family, rather than the vocation or profession, established the individual's adult identity in these societies. Individuals followed the (family) developmental trajectory through the developmental mechanisms of object relation: systemic, narcissistic, amoric, erotic, and altruistic.

In our contemporary society the attainment of full adult status through these developmental mechanisms of object relations is piecemeal, arbitrary, and inconsistent and complex, and it results in a lot of object-relations overlay (hostility and violence). Adolescents, like the aged, in many ways are outside of the productive process. They are, at the same time, a source of profit to business and a costly burden to the nuclear family, particularly where higher education is an expectation.

By definition adolescence is a transitional period between childhood and adulthood. It begins with the biological events of puberty and continues through a complex series of psychological and sociocultural events and influences in a pattern of object relations that would normally follow the path of the developmental mechanism, to the establishment of an independently functioning person. The most commonly cited landmarks of termination of adolescence include the establishment of a living situation separate from the parental home, entry into a permanent career pathway, and the increasing importance of significant relationships outside the family.

Recently, the concern of dynamic theorists has shifted from seeing the main task of adolescence as defending against the upsurge of libidinal energy and regression (Blos, 1979; Freud, 1969) and has focused instead on developmental concepts of self and identity formation, paralleling childhood development. Erik Erikson put the developmental concepts of self and identity formation into a generativity context (Friedman, 1999). Thus, the psychosocial process of adolescence identity is often conceptualized in terms of the need to address three major tasks: (1) moving from a dependent to an independent person; (2) establishing an identity; and (3) learning to relate as an adult, referred to as intimacy. Each task is addressed in adolescence in terms of object relations and the systemic, narcissistic, amoric, erotic, and altruistic developmental mechanisms, and extends into adulthood, for each must be reworked throughout the life cycle.

Upgrading Concepts of Object Relations in Adolescence

From a developmental point of view, object-relations formation seems to follow the developmental mechanisms identified earlier—systemic, narcissistic, amoric, erotic, and altruistic—which were negotiated the first time around in childhood, and then in a more extended frame of reference in adolescence.

At the *systemic* level the individual experiences object relations in *satisfaction, gratification,* and *fulfillment* when the systems work, or, in adolescence, the reworking of the systems. Some developmental theorists have characterized the early phase of what is here identified as *systemic,* as symbiotic (Mahler, Pain, & Bergman, 1975). Systemic is a broader concept, which includes the systems the child comes into the world with, or which are reworked in adolescence, and the systems that surround the child. Satisfaction is a physiological measure and relieves tension and stress; gratification is an imaginative (fantasy) value and relieves anxiety, that is, the uncertainty in ambiguity, ambivalence, and frustration; and fulfillment is an existential formulation, which relieves despair, that is, helplessness and hopelessness, with meaning and value.

Narcissistic object-relations formulations focus first on the elementary self-system of the 2-year-old child and then later at the 11- to 13-year-old level of the adolescent. Between about the ages of 11 and 13, normal adolescents become capable of what Piaget termed formal operations; that is, they can think about propositions and possibilities in object relations they have never concretely experienced, and they

can image and grasp various different future courses and consequences in the trial action of fantasy around the self in such relationships. This is a new position for the self to restructure relationships
around a self with untried possibilities. Satisfaction of this age period
will need to reshape the physiological attributes around *competence* of
the physiological self. Gratification of the self of this age period experiments with the uncertainties of the newly tried self in imagination,
where the self has to deal with ambiguity, ambivalence, and frustration, a characteristic well known in adolescents. The formulation of
meaning and value, fulfillment, at this age level, with the newly
formed self, is also very difficult.

The *amoric* period of adolescence focuses on satisfaction, gratification, and fulfillment of the romantic, idealistic, and heroic. Reworking
the 4- to 5-year-old amoric period, where family and home were the
focus of the romantic, idealistic, and heroic, 14- and 15-year-old adolescents characterize satisfaction at the physiological level of idealistic
and heroic feats. In the imagination, gratification for the adolescent of
this age level seeks out the sense of self-assertion and aggression in
romantic, idealistic, and heroic attempts to identify and belong. These
may easily be extended into hostile and violent "romantic, idealistic,
and heroic" images, as witnessed by media violence (Reiss & Roth,
1993). Finding meaning and value may draw an individual in this adolescent age group into socially positive ways to idealized or heroic ven-
tures. Or, an amoric adolescent may romanticize or idealize socially
negative object relationships that turn to hostile and violent behaviors.

The *erotic* period of adolescence is marked by mutual satisfaction,
gratification, and fulfillment. The myth of Eros recognizes the mutuality of dynamics in the trade-offs that are necessary to establish oneself in career and intimacy. These include bargains, agreements,
contracts, and covenants. Bargains are immediate arrangements that
result in satisfaction, gratification, and fulfillment. Agreements are
more extended arrangements that have rules attached. Contracts
include a penalty clause. Covenants are relationships that carry the
message "I will be with you," without other attached rules.

The story of "Jack and the Beanstalk" characterizes the trade-offs
necessary for mutual satisfaction, gratification, and fulfillment in adolescence. Jack has to steal from the adult world the bag of gold, the
magic harp, and the "goose that lays the golden egg." The bag of gold
in adolescence is the acquiring of educational and career characteris-

tics that will allow the adolescent to trade off in the marketplace of life. The magic harp identifies the talents and gifts necessary to negotiate not only interpersonal relationships but also the scenes of life. And, the goose that lays the golden egg is the integrative self that is able to formulate and dispatch such mutual trade-offs.

The *altruistic* period in adolescence focuses on the "other" as the object in terms of satisfaction, gratification, and fulfillment. Rather than engaging in the system; the self; the idealistic, romantic, and heroic; or the mutuality of the erotic period, the altruistic person can offer himself or herself for others, in object relations and caring or, as proposed by Erikson, in generativity.

From a developmental point of view, Erikson (1982) recognized adolescence as a time of forming *identity*. Identity, which became the fifth and most central state in the life cycle, emerged from the intergenerational mutuality between children in their early stages and parents and other adults at the generative stage. Unlike popularized versions of his identity concept, Erikson refused to describe it as a fixed, definite entity or quality. In his writings, he emphasizes a concept of identity as emerging from experience where an individual needs to adapt to their environment (Erikson, 1982).

For Erikson adolescence is a time for a child to form his or her identity (self) in object relations, or to lose identity in the overlay or in (self-) confusion. Aggression becomes hostility and violence when a child relinquishes his older self without either gaining a new self or when the child sustains social recognition without taking responsibility for his or her own satisfaction, gratification, and fulfillment. In identifying how aggression becomes hostility and violence in his 1942 published version of "Hitler's Imagery and German Youth," which Friedman (1999) calls a "remarkable essay," Erikson did not discuss Nazism in the context of a father with his children, but from the standpoint of a gang leader who encouraged his young delinquent male followers to repudiate the morals of their parents and neighbors. In this rapport between the Führer and German male youth (plus other not-so-young Germans who fell increasingly under his spell), an interesting development transpired. Friedman (1999) describes Erikson's view that the followers allow their identity to dissolve in exchange for social recognition. Lacking a sense of self-identity, leader and gang proclaimed to each other the validity of youthful aggression with a destructive goal over conscience and social adjustment.

SUMMARY

This study of the relationship between aggression and adolescence emphasizes a developmental model of object relations that sees assertive, aggressive, hostile, and violent behavior reflected in the object-relations mechanisms of systemic, narcissistic, amoric, erotic, and altruistic dynamics. Assertive and aggressive behaviors are evident during early childhood and again in adolescence. Rather than an inherently destructive drive in any form, these appear to be an adaptive response of the emerging self, important to both the growth and creativity of the self and its protection and security. Hostility and violence result in an overlay or complex when the dynamics of development of object relations are inhibited. Adolescence, which presents a recapitulation of the systemic, narcissistic, amoric, erotic, and altruistic mechanisms of object relations, becomes vulnerable to hostility and violence when it is cut off, as Erikson has demonstrated, from these mechanisms of object relations of so called self-identity within the context of generativity.

REFERENCES

Akhtar, S. (1996). *The birth of hatred: Developmental, clinical, and technical aspects of intense aggression*. New York: Jason Aronson.

American Psychiatric Association. (2000). *Diagnostic and statistical manual of mental disorders* (4th ed.). Washington, DC: Author.

Anderson, C.A. (1997). Effects of violent movies and trait hostility on hostile feelings, and aggressive thoughts. *Aggressive Behavior, 23,* 161–178.

Baron, R.A., & Richardson, D.R. (1994). *Human aggression* (2nd ed.). New York: Plenum.

Berkowitz, L. (1993). *Aggression: Its causes, consequences, and control.* New York: McGraw Hill.

Blos, P. (1979). *The adolescent passage: Developmental issues*. New York: International Universities Press.

Dollard, J., Miller, H., Doob, L., Mower, O., Sears, R., Ford, C., Hovland, C., & Sollenberger, R. (1939). *Frustration and aggression*. New Haven, CT: Yale University Press.

Eissler, K.R. (1978). Creativity and Adolescence. In *The Psychoanalytic study of the child* (Vol. 33, pp. 461–517). New Haven, CT: Yale University Press.

Erikson, E.H. (1982). *Identity and the life cycle*. New York: Norton.

Feinstein, S., & Giovacchini, P. (Eds.) (1976). *Adolescent psychiatry: Developmental and clinical studies* (Vol. 4). New York: Jason Aronson.

Freud, A. (1969). Adolescence. In *The writings of Anna Freud* (Vol. 5, pp. 136–166). New York: International Universities Press.

Freud, S. (1964). *Civilization and its discontent* (standard ed.). England: W.W. Norton.

Friedman, L. J. (1999). *Identity's architect: A biography of Erik H. Erikson.* New York: Scribner.

Jewett, J. (1992). *Aggression and cooperation: Helping young children develop constructive strategies.* Urbana, IL: ERIC Clearinghouse on Elementary and Early Childhood Education.

Kohut, H. (1977). *The restoration of the self.* New York: International Universities Press.

Lieberman, J. D., & Greenberg, J. (in press). Cognitive-experiential self-theory and displaced aggression. *Journal of Personality and Social Psychology.*

Lorenz, K. (1970). *Studies in animal and human behavior* (Vols. 1 and 2). Cambridge, MA: Harvard University Press.

Mahler, M. S., Pain, F., & Bergman, A. (1975). *The psychological birth of the human infant.* New York: Basic Books.

McAdams, D. P., Hart, H. M., & Maruna, S. (1998). The anatomy of generativity. In D. P. McAdams & E. de St. Aubin (Eds.), *Generativity and adult development: How and why we care for the next generation.* Washington, DC: American Psychological Association.

Moyer, K. E. (1968). Kinds of aggression and their physiological basis. *Communications in Behavioral Biology* (Part A), 65–87.

Parens, H. (1979). *The development of aggression in early childhood.* New York: Aronson.

Plaut, E. A. (1979). Play and adaptation. In A. J. Solnit, R. S. Eissler, A. Freud, M. Kris, & P. B. Neubauer (Eds.), *The psychoanalytic study of the child* (Vol. 34, pp. 217–232). New Haven, CT: Yale University Press.

Reiss, A. J., & Roth, J. A. (Eds.) (1993). *Understanding and preventing violence.* Washington, DC: National Academy Press.

Spitz, C. (1965). *The first year of life.* New York: International Universities Press.

Tomkins, S. (1978). Script theory: Differential magnification of affects. *Nebraska Symposium on Motivation, 26,* 201–263.

Werner, H. (1948). *Comparative psychology of mental development.* New York: International Universities Press.

Chapter 3

COGNITIVE PERSPECTIVE TO VIOLENCE EXPRESSION

Korrie Allen

INTRODUCTION

Children in today's society are faced with the daunting task of adjusting to a world that is no longer predictable or secure. The escalating level of youth violence in our schools and communities is capturing the nation's attention. The United States has been deemed the most violent country in the industrialized world (Fingerhut, 1993), with more than one-half of juvenile victimizations occurring at school or on school grounds (Elliot, Hamburg, & Williams, 1998). The homicide rate for adolescents doubled between the years 1984 and 1994 (Elliot et al., 1998) and is the second leading cause of death for adolescents and young adults ages 15 to 24 years.

Although the statistics sound alarming, schools are a relatively safe environment for children, compared to individual homes and neighborhoods (Elliot et al., 1998). School shootings are highly publicized; however, they affect less than 1 percent of students in our country. On the other hand violent behavior manifested in the form of intimidation and aggression toward others, often referred to as bullying, affects approximately 20 percent of the student population daily (Bastsche & Knoff, 1994). Recent statistics issued by the National Center for Victims of Crime (2002) reported an increase of violent occurrences from elementary to high school. Specifically, 74 percent of children from 8 to 11 years of age and 84 percent at the 12- to 15-year age range have reported teasing and bullying at their school.

Nearly half (45%) of elementary schools, 74 percent of middle schools, and 77 percent of high schools experience one or more violent incidents daily (e.g., bullying).

Social-emotional problems of children do not occur in a vacuum, but develop within the context of social learning and reciprocal relationships among behavioral, environmental, and personal characteristics (Bandura, 1986). It has been estimated that 25 to 30 percent of school-aged children exhibit general behavioral problems (Cowen et al., 1975). In addition, community studies indicate that between 4 and 17 percent of children in the general population meet criteria for serious emotional disturbance (Costello, Messer, Bird, Cohen, & Reinharz, 1998), and approximately 20 percent of the school-aged population qualify for a *Diagnostic and Statistical Manual of Mental Disorders* (American Psychiatric Association, 2000; DSM-IV) diagnosis (Angold, 2000).

Children who engage in violent behavior often have poor academic motivation and negative attitudes toward school, and they are more likely to drop out. Currently, 15 percent of all students aged 16 to 24 years are not enrolled in school and have not earned a high school diploma or equivalency certificate. In urban areas, the rate is as high as 35 percent. This has numerous ramifications for both the school and community. This year's class of dropouts will cost the country over 200 billion dollars during their lifetime in lost earnings and unrealized tax revenues. Students who fail to complete high school are twice as likely to receive welfare and to commit crimes that result in prison sentences. The average cost of maintaining a prisoner is at least three times higher than the annual dollars expended to educate a school-aged child.

It is sad that we have become a reactive society, intervening only when the behavior negatively impacts others. Subsequently, "our society is creating violent children and youth at a rate far faster than we could ever treat...and no single intervention strategy will solve these heterogeneous problems" (Jaffe, 1999, p. 22). Expecting one intervention program to solve the problem of violence within our schools and communities is unrealistic. As researchers continuously stress, we need to take a proactive stance and focus on interventions designed to prevent problems from emerging (Walker & Shinn, 2002). However, before we can implement population-based or preemptive interventions, we need to examine the risk factors that operate to accelerate the development of violent behavior. The reason is that the exposure to risk factors associated with violent behavior differs across specific populations, creating a heterogeneous group of at-risk youth in which the same type of intervention will not be appropriate for all children. Throughout this chapter the aim is to provide educators, mental health practitioners, and community workers with the knowledge to prevent violent behavior among at-risk youth, by examining the characteristics of the perpetrator and victim; family, developmental, and school risk factors; development of self-defeating belief systems; and a model of intervention.

DEFINING THE CHARACTERISTICS OF A BULLY AND VICTIM

The Bully (Perpetrator)

Common Behaviors of Bullies Developed by FBI

1. Greater-than-average aggressive behavior patterns.
2. The desire to dominate peers.
3. The need to feel in control and win.
4. No sense of remorse for hurting another child.
5. Refusal to accept responsibility for his or her behavior.

The perpetrator is the child who carries out a violent action. Within the school setting, violence is most often manifested in the form of bullying. Throughout this section *school violence* refers to the intimidation and threats presented by bullies and not to serious violent acts such as school shootings. Specifically, bullying is defined as an aggressive behavior repeatedly directed toward someone who is unable to or does not defend himself or herself (Hazler & Carney, 2000). There are four types of bullying: physical, verbal, social/relational, and sexual (U.S. Department of Education, 1998; Bastsche & Knoff, 1994). According to Borg (1999) the most common bullying behaviors fall under the categories of physical bullying (beating) and verbal bullying (lying and name-calling). In his book *Your Child: Bully or Victim? Understanding and Ending School Yard Tyranny*, Peter Sheras (2002) provides valuable definitions of the types of bullying. These definitions and examples are provided below to assist in the early identification of bullying.

Physical Bullying

Childhood physical aggression is often considered an early form of violence for children under 10 years old, and it is one of the strongest predictors of the development of more serious violent behaviors during
adolescence (Elliot et al., 1998). Physical bullying is the easiest form of
bullying to identify because the actions are covert. Specifically physical
bullying includes kicking, punching, hitting, pushing, and abuse on the
playground, on the bus, within the school, and on the way home from
school (Sheras, 2002). This type of bullying tends to be more common
among boys, and as children reach adolescence, the abuse becomes
more severe with the use of weapons (e.g., knives and guns).

Mike, a sixth-grade student, is a common example of a victim of
physical bullying. Mike moved to a new state over the summer and
was eager to start school and make new friends. However, from the
moment he stepped into the classroom, he was targeted by a group of
popular boys. He sat in his seat, and immediately a student grabbed
his hair and told him that he better not plan on making any new
friends. That same day on the playground, he was hit in the head with
a basketball and pushed to the ground while waiting in line to go
inside. On the bus ride home, one of the boys jumped in his seat and
began punching him in the side, informing Mike that if he told anyone about what happened he would be in the hospital. Mike went
home that evening and refused to go outside and play. His mother was
concerned because Mike loved the outdoors. The following day the
boys met Mike at the bus stop and stole his backpack and lunch
money. This continued for two weeks, and then Mike began refusing
to go to school, reporting that he felt sick. Mike's mother could not
understand what was going on, Mike had always enjoyed school, and
she knew that he was not sick. She made Mike go to school, but for-
got to give him lunch money. At the bus stop, the bullies thought
Mike was trying to fool them and began hitting him, but this time hit
him in the face. When Mike arrived at school, his nose and lips were
bleeding. He was sent to the office, and when his mother came to get
him he began crying and explained how hard the last two weeks had
been.

This is a common example of physical bullying, and some of the
early warning signs were Mike's change in behavior and refusal to go
to school. This is an example of how important it is to be aware of
children's nonverbal signals. Specifically, Mike changed from an extro-
verted child to a withdrawn and depressed one.

Verbal Bullying

Verbal bullying includes name-calling, taunts, threats, and gossip used to purposely hurt others. Verbal abuse is the most frequent type of bullying, but is the most overlooked and ignored by adults (Sheras, 2002). This type of bullying tends to be most popular amongst girls. Primarily middle-school–aged girls understand the power of their words, which they use to manipulate, gossip, and hurt others. Although these children are only using words, verbal bullying negatively affects the student's self-concept and confidence.

Shoshannah, an eighth-grade girl, has an elongated tongue that causes her to slur her words and speak slower than most of the other students. A group of classmates tease her daily, calling her such names as "retard, drunken talker, fagot, and moron." When she is called on during a lecture, the moment she opens her mouth they begin to laugh. Consequently, Shoshannah has stopped talking within the school building. She refuses to speak to other students in the hallways and begs her teachers not to ask her questions in front of the other students. She now refuses to go to school, frequently complaining of stomach problems and headaches.

This is an example of the negative impact verbal bullying can have on a child or adolescent. Some of the early warning signs were Shoshannah's failing grades and limited friendships. In addition, she displayed symptoms characteristic of depression and anxiety.

Social/Relational Bullying

Social abuse includes "deliberate shunning, rejection, ostracism, and cruel practical jokes" (Sheras, 2002, p. 43). Social/relational bullies try to convince their peers to exclude or reject a certain person and cut the victims off from their social connection. The child who sits alone at lunch, never leaves home on the weekend, and has no friend is often the victim of social bullying. This type of bullying is connected to verbal bullying and tends to occur when children (most often girls) spread rumors about others or exclude an ex-friend from the peer group.

Jennifer's family recently moved from southern California to the Midwest. In California Jennifer had many friends and excelled on the soccer and basketball teams. She was excited to begin her new school, but from the moment she stepped through the door she felt uncomfortable. The girls in her classes ignored her, and when she was asked to work in groups she never had a partner. The worst harassment occurred during lunch in the cafeteria. She sat alone and was the center of numerous jokes. The popular girls laughed and teased her, and on two occasions they threw ice-cream sandwiches in her hair.

Jennifer tried to stay positive, and she looked forward to the soccer season. However, the same girls played on the team and continued to tease and exclude her from activities. They told her the wrong practice times and stole her uniform from the locker room. Jennifer attempted to explain the situation to her parents, but they had difficulty believing children could act in such a manner. Following the next soccer game, Jennifer's mother invited the girls to her house for a sleepover. During dinner the girls openly teased Jennifer about her clothes and home. After an hour her mother asked the girls to leave.

Social bullying negatively impacts academic performance, school attendance, and self-concept. Jennifer's parents eventually sent her to a private school, where she enjoyed social and academic success. Unfortunately, for many children that is not an option, and they must endure the daily teasing and social ostracism.

Bullying has been the most dominant form of school violence witnessed and experienced within American schools (Hazler & Carney, 2000). The type of school violence experienced increases in severity and intensity as children progress from elementary to middle school and then from middle to high school (Furlong, 2000). The violence tends to begin with teasing and bullying at the elementary level, next increases to more antisocial and aggressive behaviors such as fighting, then to fatal and traumatic aggressive and violent acts such as weapon use (Furlong, 2000). Bullying can take the form of a cycle in which the bullied may feel compelled to retaliate on the bullies and fight back, bring weapons to school, or commit suicide (U.S. Department of Education, 1998). It would be highly beneficial if interventions were afforded to both the bully and the bullied in order to prevent this cycle from occurring.

Reasons to Take Action (www.bullybeware.com)

1. Sixty percent of identified bullies have a criminal conviction by the age of 24 years.
2. Bullying occurs once every seven minutes.
3. The majority of bullying occurs in or close to school buildings.

4. Primary-aged children who were labeled by their peers as bullies required more support as adults from government agencies, had more court convictions, had a greater incidence of alcoholism, were more likely to have an antisocial personality, and used more mental health services.

5. Only 25 percent of students report that teachers intervene in bullying situations, whereas 71 percent of teachers believe they always intervene.

The Victim

Throughout the past decade, there has been a decline in students' perception of school safety, particularly in unsupervised areas (i.e., cafeterias, playgrounds, etc.) as a result of the increase in reports of school violence. As indicated earlier, serious and traumatic acts of school violence such as shootings are relatively rare; however, these incidents have affected children's perception of school safety. School violence affects many variables, which interact to affect a child's academic performance. The sense of safety enables a child to focus his or her attention on school material rather than on the behaviors of his or her peers. According to Furlong's (2000) recent investigations, 4 to 5 percent of middle school students missed one day of school a month due to concerns about school safety.

School violence and the perception of safety have both short- and long-term effects. The short-term consequences of bullying or the fear of bullying will negatively impact children's interactions with peers, style of dress, verbal expression, and the way they present themselves in school (Furlong, 2000). The long-term effects of peer victimization, specifically bullying, include low self-esteem (Egan & Perry, 1998; Hazler & Carney, 2000); depression (Hazler & Carney, 2000; Hodges & Perry, 1999; Mazza & Overstreet, 2000); isolation (Bastsche & Knoff, 1994; Hodges & Perry, 1999; Leff, Power, Manz, Costigan, & Nabors, 2001); school avoidance (Kochenderfer & Ladd, 1996) and truancy or dropping out due to fears; and peer relationship problems (Leff et al., 2001). Victims of school violence may also demonstrate aggressive and antisocial behaviors (Bastsche & Knoff, 1994; Fryxell & Smith, 2000; Hazler & Carney, 2000; Mazza & Overstreet, 2000), suicidal behaviors (Mazza & Street, 2000), and social anxiety (Hazler & Carney, 2000; Hodges & Perry, 1999), and their risk taking within their personal lives and with their careers may also be affected (Leff et al., 2001). Researchers maintain that bullied students tend to have poor psychosocial adjustment when compared to peers (see Nansel et al., 2001). Due to the adverse effects of bullying, it is not enough to simply understand the characteristics of the perpetrator and victim. To prevent bullying, professionals working with children must understand the risk factors associated with violent behavior because different developmental pathways cause similar behavior, suggesting that the same type of intervention will not be appropriate for all children (Frick, Bodin, & Barry, 2000).

RISK FACTORS ASSOCIATED WITH VIOLENT BEHAVIOR

The number of children demonstrating various forms of behavioral and emotional maladjustment has been increasing since the 1960s (Bernard & Joyce, 1984). Unfortunately, many children are exposed to environmental risk factors that negatively impact development, and it is the accumulation of these risk factors that increases the likelihood a child will engage in violent behavior. To aid in the early identification of an "at-risk" youth and prevent the onset of severe emotional and behavioral disorders, mental health practitioners, teachers, and other professionals working with children must recognize the risk factors that may predispose children to violent behavior.

Family Environment

Violence is a multifaceted problem in which the social and cultural environment tends to either promote or buffer violence, and the "environmental characteristics can either exacerbate or ameliorate its impact on children and families" (Fick, Osofsky, & Lewis, 1997, p. 263). Aggressive, impulsive, and violent behavior is the end result of a complex interaction among many different types of causal mechanisms, including individual vulnerabilities (e.g., poor impulse control or low intelligence), problems in their rearing environment (e.g., poor parental discipline or psychopathology in parents), and stressors in their larger social ecology (e.g., living in poor, high-crime neighborhoods or having poor educational opportunities) (Frick et al., 2000). A significant risk factor for increased violence exposure and victimization is living in poverty (American Psychological Association, 1993). Currently, the problem is increasing, with almost one-fourth (23%) of

American children living in poverty (Fick et al., 1997). Due to increased stress, low-income parents are often more inclined to use harsh and punitive methods of discipline with minimal positive reinforcement and warmth. Ineffective parenting practices such as failure to monitor and supervise, harsh and inconsistent discipline practices, and little positive involvement with children negatively impact their development.

The child may model this type of behavior, and carry it into the school setting. These behaviors usually stem from homes where physical punishment is the primary form of discipline. These parents tend to be unsupportive and rejecting, have poor problem-solving skills and model aggressive behaviors as a means to gain control over a situation (Roberts & Morotti, 2000). Bandura was one of the first to address this issue with his famous 1963 "Bobo Doll" experiments, which revealed that children learn directly from watching others model behavior and then imitate the learned behavior. According to Bandura's social learning theory, children learn aggressive behaviors as well as the consequences by witnessing the consequences of the modeled aggressive behavior (Rutherford & Nelson, 1995). Bulliers will exhibit the behaviors they have learned to successfully attain their goals (Rutherford & Nelson, 2000). If these children are consistently exposed to this type of problem-solving technique, it is what they will utilize when away from the home, due to their limited ability to generate modeled alternatives (Roberts & Morotti, 2000).

Developmental Factors

Wittmer (1993) found (cited in Vernon, 1997, p. 11) that many children in the United States are exposed to the following serious problems, which may have a devastating impact on their development:

- Every 47 seconds, a child is abused or neglected.
- Every 7 minutes, a child is killed or injured by guns.
- Every day 6 teenagers commit suicide.
- Every 14 hours, a child younger than five is murdered.
- Every 5 hours, a 15- to 19-year-old is murdered.
- Every 4 seconds of the school day, a public school student is corporally punished.

- Every 26 seconds, a child runs away from home.
- Every day 100,000 children are homeless.
- Every day 2,989 American children experience divorce in their families.
- Every 74 seconds, a 15- to 19-year-old woman has an abortion.

As professionals working with children, we have become increasingly aware of the need to help children cope with normal life stressors as well as with the more serious familial and socio-emotional problems that often result in self-defeating behaviors such as substance abuse, suicide, teen pregnancy, and violence (Vernon, 1997, 1993; Wittmer, 1993).

In addition, to biological risk factors such as prematurity, low birth weight, prenatal brain damage, low intelligence, and disability, these causal mechanisms often have a devastating impact on child development. Specifically, Perry (1997) has conducted extensive research on children reared in violent settings and found that these children often experience neglect or traumatic stress, which negatively impacts development. Furthermore, Perry states, "the combination of a lack of critical emotional experiences and persisting traumatic stress leads to a dramatic alteration in the brain's modulation and regulation capacity...which is characterized by an over development of brainstem and midbrain neurophysiology and functions (e.g., anxiety, impulsivity, poor affect regulation, motor hyperactivity) and an underdevelopment of limbic and cortical neurophysiology and functions (e.g., empathy, problem-solving skills) predisposing the child to aggressive and violent behavior" (Perry, 1997, p. 138). Therefore, when confronted with a conflict, children exposed to violence may use the more primitive parts of their brain, causing them to be more reactive, reflexive and limited in their ability to use higher-level or developmentally appropriate cognitive solutions (Perry, 1997).

Over the last 25 years, there has been a wide range of data that indicates problem-solving and coping skills play an adaptive role in dealing with stressful life events and psychological adjustment in general (Heppner, Lee, Pretorious, Wang, & Wei, 2002); without the ability to formulate alternative responses, these children are at a serious disadvantage when confronted with a conflict. Research on children who are aggressive and impulsive has consistently documented deficits in the way they process social information, including the way they encode social cues, interpret these cues, develop social goals, develop appropriate responses, decide on appropriate responses, and enact appropriate responses (Crick & Dodge, 1994). Thus, when working with so-called at-risk children it is imperative to assess their coping and problem-solving skills, as they may have failed to develop appropriate cognitions and emotional affect. It is important to note that not all children reared in a hostile environment become violent; rather, it is the accumulation of risk factors that predisposes them to violent behavior.

Risk Factors within the School Setting

Professionals working with children and adolescents need to develop an understanding of the behaviors that may indicate exposure to violence, such as inattention in class; underachievement or academic failure; isolation from the peer group; and provocative acts, clowning, aggression, and oppositional behavior (Marans & Schaefer, 1998). Although schools and community agencies do not have a direct impact on familial risk factors, a positive environment may offset the negative effects of risk factors (Walker & Shinn, 2002). Walker and Shinn (2002) emphasize that "it is very important for educators to include a specific analysis of the risk and protective factors potentially operating in a vulnerable child's life upon entering school" (p. 10). Schools are embedded within communities, and in many ways they reflect community-level processes. For example, schools in urban, poor, disorganized communities experience much more violence than do schools in rural, affluent, organized communities. Once a child begins school, educators and parents share the responsibility of shaping the student's behavior (Gottfredson, 2001). The school discipline policy, teacher-student relations, and student's attitude toward school and peers may prevent the development of violent behavior.

According to Rutherford and Nelson (1995), there are three possible explanations for why youth demonstrate aggressive behavior(s) while in school. First, due to the possible hostile home environment these children experience, they are likely to be vigilant of their surroundings and may experience difficulty with discriminating cues emitted from the environment. They may, in turn, interpret a neutral situation as a threatening one and respond using aggressive behaviors (Lennon, 2001; Rutherford & Nelson, 2000). Second, bulliers may be reinforced for aggressive behavior through attention gained and the avoidance of things they find aversive, unpleasant, or undesirable (i.e., working on a subject they find difficult). Finally, children may exhibit violent and aggressive behaviors if it will gain them approval in their social group at school (Rutherford & Nelson, 1995).

Research documents that promoting healthy relationships and environments is more effective in reducing school misconduct and crime than is instituting punitive penalties. Peers and teachers who speak to students can often provide the most useful information when students are in trouble (Mulvey & Cauffman, 2001). Unfortunately, the national policy response to youth violence has been one of harsh punishment of children and adolescents. Elliot et al. (1998) indicate that rates of incarceration have been rapidly rising and that children as young as 10 years old can be tried as adults and, if convicted, jailed with adults. These policies are extremely expensive and unsuccessful in deterring crime or decreasing recidivism. Rather than establishing a supportive and positive school environment, most school districts have followed the national policy and developed a zero-tolerance policy. This type of system hinders student and staff relations, causing children and adolescents to avoid sharing information. In many of the inner-city school systems, students must pass security inspections that involve metal detectors and X-ray machines. Security guards have assumed the role of disciplinarian within the school, while teachers are solely responsible for academics. With this sort of shift in the paradigm, teachers are rarely establishing relationships with the students who need the most attention (Devine, 1996).

Furthermore, Resnick and colleagues (1997) indicate that the most powerful predictor of adolescent well-being is a feeling of connection to the school. Students who feel close to others, fairly treated, and devoted to school are less likely to engage in risky behaviors than those who feel rejected. The school climate may either lessen or compound the risk factors that children bring to the classroom (Reinke & Herman, 2002). Rutter and colleagues (1997) found that schools with systematic discipline procedures, good teacher-child relationships, and structured reward systems for appropriate behavior have fewer incidents of violent behavior. Conversely, school settings that use inconsistent or arbitrary rules, have low expectations for student performance, and show inattention to violent behavior tend to foster delinquent behavior. Effective solutions to school violence require comprehensive programs that involve teacher, parent, and school cooperation.

EARLY IDENTIFICATION

In order to create the sense of security for students that schools used to hold, early identification of both perpetrators and victims of school violence is imperative. Similar to most problems within society, ranging from medical to marital problems, the earlier the intervention is implemented, the better the outcome. There is a pattern of a sharp increase in delinquency and crime beginning at ages 13 to 14 that peaks at about age 18 and steeply declines for serious forms of violence after age 21 (Elliot, 1994). Violent/aggressive behaviors begin early, and the possibility that these behaviors will evolve into more severe and possibly fatal behaviors can be reduced or eliminated.

There are many warning signs that parents and school professionals can be aware of that can help identify a child who has the potential of developing severe violent behaviors. Furlong, Morrison, Chung, Bates, and Morrison (1997) discuss the results of research performed by Walker, Colvin, and Ramsey (1995), where they found that most students who commit violent acts have a distinct profile. For instance, most peer perpetrators within the school are male; experience difficulty with peers, social skills, and academics; and have a prior history of antisocial and aggressive behavior.

The United States Department of Education (Dwyer & Osher, 2000) composed a list of various signs that may aid in the early identification of more pronounced or frequent antisocial and violent behaviors within students. Of these signs, there are many that can be identified in an elementary, middle, and high school student, including social withdrawal; excessive feelings of isolation and rejection; experiencing peer victimization; feelings of being picked on or persecuted; and low interest in school as well as poor academic performance. Students may express violence in writing and drawings, uncontrolled anger, patterns of impulsive and frequent hitting, and bullying behaviors. A history of discipline and aggressive behavior may also help in the identification of the emergence of violent behavior. Some warning signs, which may be helpful in the identification of potential violent behavior in middle school or high school students, include intolerance for differences, prejudicial attitudes, drug and alcohol use, affiliation with gangs, possession of and use of firearms, and serious threats of violence. Moreover, youths who have school and conduct problems are more likely than their better-adjusted peers to own a gun (O'Donnell, 1995; Pepler & Slaby, 1993).

Students, school professionals, and mental health practitioners alike will benefit from having an understanding of and the ability to recognize these early warning signs exhibited by students (Burns, Dean, & Jacob-Timm, 2001). This will aid school professionals in the process of reduction and prevention of such behaviors and from mislabeling a student as exhibiting or not exhibiting aggressive or violent behaviors.

DEVELOPMENT AND IDENTIFICATION OF MALADAPTIVE OR SELF-DEFEATING BELIEF SYSTEMS

Although many children are exposed to environmental risk factors, the children who become violent offenders tend to have maladaptive beliefs systems and emotional and behavioral regulation. As previously indicated, the exposure to risk factors may predispose a child to violent behavior; however, cognitions are often the mediational variables by which these external factors have their effect (DiGiuseppe, 1988). Therefore, children's disturbed emotions and self-defeating behaviors are often generated by their irrational or dysfunctional beliefs. Children labeled as at-risk tend to overgeneralize, taking one negative aspect and creating global judgments of self-worth (Bernard & Cronan, 1999). For example, a mistake on a test could yield the beliefs that "If something does not happen the way it should, it's my fault and I must be perfect." Bernard and Joyce (1984) suggest that this thinking can be equated to Piaget's developmental notion of conservation and assimilation. Thus, this thinking, in turn, also reflects a cognitive inability to hold a positive value of oneself in the face of contradictory information. As the children mature, they can better identify their thoughts and the connection to the emotional disturbance, and subsequently the irrational thoughts can be effectively challenged (Bernard & Joyce, 1984). Consequently, it is imperative for youth-serving professionals to teach at-risk children more adaptive and self-helping modes of thinking and problem solving.

You may be wondering how this applies to violent behavior in children. Let us take the example of an 11-year-old fifth-grader, Raheem. Raheem has been attending the same school for two years. During lunch he sits alone, and the same group of children sit at the table next to him. He assumes that when someone looks in his direction, they are making fun of him. Raheem is thinking "these kids are talking bad about me and must not like me, and it is terrible not to be liked," and subsequently he feels angry. Raheem has drawn inferences about the children's behavior. The moment one of the students begins to tease him, he punches him in the mouth. This chain of events occurs almost on a daily basis, and Raheem has not conceptualized that this reaction only decreases his chance of making friends. Raheem's irrational beliefs will continue to yield maladaptive emotional and behavioral responses. Simply removing Raheem from the lunchroom or changing his lunch period will not alleviate the problem. Raheem has developed a self-defeating belief system, which negatively impacts his ability to effectively cope and problem-solve when confronted with a difficult situation.

Although there may be different causal mechanisms, the development of maladaptive or self-defeating belief systems yields poor behavioral and emotional regulation. Prior to beginning to use cognitive behavioral strategies, it is important to identify the developmental level of the child and environmental factors that may have impeded cognitive development. As indicated in the previous sections, Perry (1997) demonstrates that living in a violent environment often negatively impacts the child's ability to use higher-level thinking skills. Consequently, some practitioners have questioned the use of cognitive therapy with younger children because of their developmental limitations. However, over 20 years ago, DiGiuseppe, Miller, and Trexler (1979) found that elementary school children are capable of acquiring knowledge of rational-emotive principles and that modification of a child's self-verbalizations or irrational self-statements can have a positive effect on emotional adjustment of behavior (p. 225).

Regardless of how an emotional disturbance is learned, it is important to focus on the cognitive structures and behaviors that maintain the disturbance. Specifically, the ABC Model of Rational Emotive Behavior Therapy (REBT) indicates that negative life events we confront are called Activating Events (A's), and the emotions or behavior that follow are called the Consequences (C's). Although people often attribute the cause of their current distress to the Activating Event in their life, REBT holds that it is their thoughts and beliefs (B's) about Activating Events that more directly cause their disturbances.

Rational beliefs tend to be consistent with objective reality, expressed conditionally, and to lead to self-enhancing emotions and goal-directed behaviors. Irrational beliefs are generally distortions of reality, expressed in absolute terms, and lead to inappropriate feelings that often block goal attainment.

1. It's awful if others do not like me.
2. I am bad if I make a mistake.
3. Everything should go my way, and I should always get what I want.
4. Things should come easily for me.
5. The world should be fair and bad people punished.
6. I should not show my feelings.
7. Adults should be perfect.
8. There's only one right answer.
9. I must win.
10. I should not have to wait for anything.

The Most Common Irrational Beliefs of Children (Waters, 1982)

1. List sensible versus nonsensible thoughts.
2. List thoughts, and have children rate thoughts as true/false or rational/irrational.
3. Play tic-tac-toe with fact and beliefs statements.
4. Play Draw-a-Feeling game: have the child draw a picture and label the feeling.

Detecting Children's Irrational Beliefs in a Classroom Setting (Waters, 1982)

When working with children and adolescents, it is important to focus on the presence of maladaptive, illogical, and irrational cognitions, and to work to restructure self-defeating beliefs systems in an effort to reduce the suffering of the child and prevent the occurrence of future problems. Often someone working with at-risk children links their behavior to a continuum of severity that includes children who have minimal behavioral problems to those with severe emotional and behavioral problems. In addition, the onset of violent behavior can occur over a period of time or as an immediate response to a stressful life event. Therefore, intervention programs must be multifaceted and service a range of problems. This idea is reflected in Walker and Shinn (2002), who present an intervention model similar to that found in public health in which they emphasize promoting positive development and preventing problems of at-risk children and adolescents.

INTERVENTIONS

Prior to implementing an intervention program, it is imperative to gather information from children, parents, school personnel, and community workers about their perception of violence in the school and community settings. Then, based on the information obtained, an intervention curriculum can be developed or adopted to meet the needs of the people within the school and community. Combining school-based and family-focused interventions can positively influence these two primary socializing environments of youth in a synergistic manner, building youth competencies and enhancing positive youth development and reducing behavioral problems (Spoth, Redmond, Trudeau, & Shin, 2002). The most effective interventions use a multidisciplinary approach that takes into account the differences in individual stages of development, families, peer groups, schools, and community environments (Elliot et al., 1998).

In an effort to promote prevention aimed at reducing violent behavior, youth-serving professionals have adopted a public health framework in which universal interventions are delivered to an entire population. This type of integrated model illustrated by Walker and Shinn (2002) encompasses three levels of prevention: primary, secondary, and tertiary. Specifically, primary preventions aim to reduce the likelihood that problems will emerge, whereas secondary preventions aim to reverse harm from exposure to known risk factors, and tertiary preventions attempt to reduce the harm experienced by the most severely involved individuals. By employing primary prevention strategies, it is expected that the adjustment problems of 75 to 85 percent of a school's students can be prevented, whereas the majority of the remaining students should respond to secondary preventions, and the few remaining would require a more complex tertiary prevention strategy (Walker & Shinn, 2002).

Primary prevention strategies are universally implemented with the aim of preventing dysfunctional behavior from emerging. One of most widely used school-based curriculums is the *Promoting Alternative Thinking Strategies Program* (PATHS) developed by Kusche and Greenberg (1995), which includes 57 lessons administered by the classroom teacher. The lessons range from 25 to 30 minutes and include class discussions, directed instruction, modeling, and videotaped segments. The goal of the program is to help children develop appropriate problem-solving, self-control, and emotional regulation skills. Recent research found a modest positive effect for participants at the end of the first grade on peer sociometric measures of aggression and hyperactive-disruptive disorders (Leff et al., 2001). Recently the PATHS program was integrated into the FAST Track Project and continues to have positive results.

An additional universal prevention program is the Second Step Program (Grossman et al., 1997), which includes both school- and home-based components. The Second Step Program teaches prosocial behavior by focusing on improving empathy, impulse control, problem solving, and anger management/conflict resolution (Walker & Shinn, 2002). The program includes 30 classroom lessons ranging from 35 to 45 minutes. Research on the program found that students exhibited less physical aggression and more neutral or prosocial behaviors in the lunchroom and on the playground than the students in the control condition (Leff et al., 2001).

Overall, the aim of primary prevention is to provide violence prevention strategies, effective academic instruction, and schoolwide behavior expectations in an effort to limit the emergence of violent behavior (Walker et al., 1996). On the other hand, secondary prevention includes students that are more severely at-risk, requiring additional services such as mentoring, behavioral or academic support, and skill development (Walker & Shinn, 2002). These interventions focus on small groups and individual students who fail to respond to the primary preventions. The most efficacious prevention program that targets high-risk disruptive and aggressive kindergartners is the First Step to Success Program (Walker et al., 1997, 1998). This program consists of three components: (1) comprehensive screening procedure to identify at-risk students, (2) school-based intervention promoting prosocial school behavior, and (3) home-based intervention to improve parenting skills and communication between home and school. Recent longitudinal investigations indicate that behavioral gains produced by First Step in kindergarten were maintained into the upper elementary grades (as cited in Walker & Shinn, 2002).

Secondary prevention serves at-risk children for problem behavior in an effort to reverse the harm of exposure to risk factors, whereas the third level of prevention, tertiary, aims to reduce the harm of behavior problems for students already identified with behavioral problems. The Fast Tract Project provides seven integrated interventions programs to treat high-risk kindergarten students (Conduct Problems

Prevention Research Group, 1999). Specifically, the students with severe behavior problems are targeted, and they receive individual, home, and community services. The programs provided are the PATHS curriculum, parent groups, child social skills training groups, parent-child sharing time, home visiting, child-peer pairing and academic tutoring. Recent investigations demonstrated positive outcomes for the children's social cognition, reading, and social skills, and in addition, parenting skills improved.

Prevention is the aim of mental health practitioners, school personnel, and community workers. Clearly, primary prevention is the overall goal, and schools that employ such interventions will provide a positive environment for their students. By adopting this model throughout the country, primarily in the inner-city schools, where there tends to be more exposure to risk factors, the number of students who have difficulty adjusting to behavioral, social, and academic demands would be reduced. Most important, prevention must take place across environments to have the greatest impact.

CONCLUSION

Violence is a serious problem that demoralizes our schools, families, and communities. We have reviewed the characteristics of a bully and victim, as well as the risk factors, early identification, and intervention strategies that may be employed with at-risk youth. The goal as professionals who serve youth is to reduce the probability that the at-risk child will become a violent offender. Further expansion of this topic is found in chapter 7, "Bullying and Aggression among Youth" (Galezewski). Implementing school-based intervention programs is an appropriate method of primary prevention. However, when working with students who exhibit severe behavior problems, we must combine school- and community-based interventions. Successful intervention programs include many systems that impact the child, whereas delinquency programs target only one behavior and setting (Zigler, Taussig, & Black, 1992). Efforts to intervene with children who have become violent offenders are a much greater cost to society than are prevention efforts. In chapter 8, Klco discusses "Forensic Issues and Violence Prevention Programming." The importance of prevention is not a new revelation; health care and mental health professionals and school personnel have advocated for prevention and documented its potential. As youth-serving professionals, we need to begin taking the necessary steps to prevent children from becoming violent offenders in our homes, schools, and communities.

REFERENCES

American Psychiatric Association. (2000). *Diagnostic and statistical manual of mental disorders* (4th ed.). Washington, DC: Author.

American Psychological Association, Commission on Violence and Youth. (1993). *Violence and youth: Psychology's response: Vol. 1. Summary report.* Washington, DC.

Angold, A., Costello, E. J., Burns, B. J., Erkanli, A., & Farmer, E. M. Z. (2000). Effectiveness of non-residential specialty mental health services for children and adolescents in the "real world." *Journal of the American Academy of Child and Adolescent Psychiatry, 39,* 154–160.

Bandura A. (1986). *Social foundations of thought and action.* Englewood Cliffs, NJ: Prentice-Hall.

Bastsche, G. M., & Knoff, H. M. (1994). Bullies and their victims: Understanding a pervasive problem in the schools. *School Psychology Review, 23*(2), 165–174.

Bernard, M. E., & Cronan, F. (1999). The child and adolescent scale of irrationality: Validation data and mental health correlates. *Journal of Cognitive Psychotherapy: An International Quarterly, 13,* 121–133.

Bernard, M. E., & Joyce, M. R. (1984). *Rational-emotive therapy with children and adolescents.* New York: Wiley Press.

Borg, M. G. (1999). The emotional reactions of school bullies and their victims. *Educational Psychology, 18,* 433–444.

Burns, M. K., Dean, V. J., & Jacob-Timm, S. (2001). Assessment of violence potential among school children: Beyond profiling. *Psychology in the Schools, 38*(3), 239–247.

Conduct Problems Prevention Research Group. (1999). Initial impact of the fast track prevention trial of conduct problems: I. The high risk sample. *Journal of Consulting and Clinical Psychology, 67,* 631–647.

Costello, E. J., Messer, S. C., Bird, H. R., Cohen, P., & Reinharz, H. (1998). The prevalence of serious emotional disturbance: A re-analysis of community studies. *Journal of Child and Family Studies, 7,* 411–432.

Cowen, E., Trost, L., Lorion, R., Door, E., Izzo, B. L., & Issaacson, J. (1975). Evaluation of a preventively oriented, school based mental health program. *Psychology in the Schools, 12,* 161–166.

Crick, N. R., & Dodge, K. A. (1994). A review and reformulation of social information-processing mechanisms in children's social adjustment. *Psychological Bulletin, 115,* 74–101.

Devine, J. F. (1996). *Maximum security: The culture of inner-city schools.* Chicago, IL: University of Chicago Press.

DiGiuseppe, R. (1988). A cognitive behavior approach to the treatment of conduct disordered children and adolescents. In N. Epstein, S. Schlesinger, & W. Dryden (Eds.), *Cognitive behavioral therapy with families* (pp. 183–214). New York: Brunner/Mazal.

Dwyer, K., & Osher, D. (2000). *Safeguarding our children: An action guide.* Washington, DC: U.S. Departments of Education and Justice, American Institutes for Research.

Egan, S. K., & Perry, D. G. (1998). Does low self-regard invite victimization? *Developmental Psychology, 34*(2), 299–309.

Elliot, D. S. (1994). Youth violence: An overview. *Congressional Program: Children and Violence, 9*(2), 15–20.

Elliot, D. S., Hamburg, B. A., & Williams, K. R. (1998). Violence in American schools: An overview. In D. S. Elliot, B. A. Hamburg, & K. R. Williams (Eds.), *Violence in American schools* (pp. 3–28). New York: Cambridge University Press.

Fick, A. C., Osofsky, J. D., & Lewis, M. L. (1997). Perceptions of violence: Children, parents, and police officers. In J. D. Osofsky (Ed.), *Children in a violent society* (pp. 261–276). New York: Guilford Press.

Fingerhut, L. A. (1993). Firearm mortality among children, youth, and young adults 1–34 years of age, trends and current status: United States, 1985–1990. In *Advance data from vital health statistics* (no. 231). Hyattsville, MD: National Center for Health Statistics.

Frick, P. J., Bodin, D. S., & Barry, C. T. (2000). Psychopathic traits and conduct problems in community and clinic-referred samples of children: Further development of the Psychopathy Screening Device. *Psychological Assessment, 4,* 382–393.

Furlong, M. (2000). The school in school violence: Definitions and facts. *Journal of Emotional and Behavioral Disorders, 8*(2), 71–82.

Furlong, M. L., Morrison, G. M., Chung, A., Bates, M., & Morrison, R. (1997). School violence: A multicomponent reduction strategy. In G. Bear (Ed.), *Children's needs: Psychological perspectives II.* Arlington, VA: National Association of School Psychologists.

Gottfredson, D. C. (2001). *Schools and delinquency.* New York: Cambridge Press.

Grossman, D. C., Neckerman, H. J., Koepsell, T. D., Liu, P. Y., Asher, K. N., Beland, K., Frey, K., & Rivara, F. P. (1997). Effectiveness of a violence prevention curriculums among children in elementary school: A randomized controlled trial. *Journal of the American Medical Association, 277,* 1065–1611.

Hazler, R. J., & Carney, J. V. (2000). When victims turn aggressors: Factors in the development of deadly school violence. *Professional School Counseling, 4*(2), 105–112.

Heppner, P., Lee, D., Pretorious, T. B., Wang, Y. W., & Wei, M. (2002). Examining the generalizability of problem-solving appraisal in black

South Africans. *Journal of Consulting and Clinical Psychology, 49*(4), 484–498.

Hodges, E.V.E., & Perry, D.G. (1999). Personal and interpersonal antecedents and consequences of victimization by peers. *Journal of Personality and Social Psychology, 76*(4), 677–685.

Jaffe, P.G. (1999). Why changing the YOA does not impact youth crime developing effective prevention programs for children and adolescents. *Canadian Psychology, 40,* 22–38.

Kochenderfer, B.J., & Ladd, G.W. (1996). Peer victimization: Manifestations and relations to school adjustment in kindergarten. *Journal of School Psychology, 34*(3), 267–283.

Kusche, C.A., & Greenberg, M.T. (1995). *The PATHS curriculum.* Seattle: Developmental Research and Programs.

Leff, S.S., Power, T.J., Manz, P.H., Costigan, T.E., & Nabors, L.A. (2001). School-based aggression prevention programs for young children: Current status and implications for violence prevention. *School Psychology Review, 30*(3), 344–362.

Marans, S., & Schaefer, M. (1998). Community policing, schools, and mental health: The challenge of collaboration. In D.S. Elliot, B.A. Hamburg, & K.R. Williams (Eds.), *Violence in American schools* (pp. 3–28). New York: Cambridge University Press.

Mazza, J.J., & Overstreet, S. (2000). Children and adolescents exposed to community violence: A mental health perspective for school psychologists. *School Psychology Review, 29*(1), 86–101.

Miller, G., & Rubin, K. (1999, Spring). Victimization of school-aged children. *Communiqué* [Special edition], pp. 8–13.

Mulvey, E.P., & Cauffman, E. (2001). The inherent limits of predicting school violence. *American Psychologist, 56*(10), 797–802.

Nansel, T.R., Overpeck, M.O., Pilla, R.S., Ruan, J.W., Simmons-Morton, B., & Scheidt, P. (2001). Bullying behaviors among US youth: Prevalence and association with psychosocial adjustment. *Journal of the American Medical Association, 285*(16), 2094–2100.

National Center for Victims of Crime. (2002). *Teen Victim Project.* Available Internet: http://www.ncvc.org.

National Crime and Prevention Council. (1997). *Preventing crime by investing in families: Promoting positive outcomes in children six to twelve years old.* Ottawa, ON: Ministry of Justice.

O'Donnell, C.R. (1995). Firearms death among children and youth. *American Psychologist, 50*(9), 782–788.

Pepler, D., & Slaby, R.G. (1993). *Violence and youth: Psychology's response. Summary report of the APA Commission on violence and youth.* (Commission on Violence and Youth, Ed.). Washington, DC: American Psychological Association.

Perry, B. D. (1997). Incubated in terror: Neurodevelopmental factors in the "Cycle of Violence." In J. D. Osofsky (Ed.), *Children in a violent society* (pp. 124–149). New York: Guilford Press.

Reinke, W. M., & Herman, K. C. (2002). A research agenda for school violence prevention: Comment. *American Psychologist, 57,* 796–797.

Resnick, M. D., Bearman, P. S., Blum, R. W., Bauman, K. E., Harris, K. M., & Jones, J. (1997). Protecting adolescents from harm: Finding from the National Longitudinal Study on Adolescent Health. *Journal of the American Medical Association, 278,* 823–832.

Roberts, W. J., Jr., & Morotti, A. A. (2000). The bully as victim: Understanding bully behaviors to increase the effectiveness of interventions in the bully-victim dyad. *Professional School Counseling, 4*(2), 148–156.

Rutherford, R. B., & Nelson, C. M. (1995). Management of aggressive and violent behavior in the schools. *Focus on Exceptional Children, 27,* 1–15.

Rutter, M., Maughan, B., Meyer, J., Pickles, A., Silberg, J., Simonoff, E., & Taylor, E. (1997). Heterogeneity of antisocial behavior: Causes, continuities, and consequences. In D. W. Osgood (Ed.), *Motivation and delinquency* (pp. 45–118). Lincoln: University of Nebraska Press.

Sheras, P. (2002). *Your child: Bully or victim? Understanding and ending school yard tyranny.* New York: Skylight Book Press.

Spoth, R. L., Redmond, C., Trudeau, L., & Shin, C. (2002). Longitudinal substance initiation outcomes for a universal preventative intervention program combining family and school programs. *Psychology of Addictive Behaviors, 16,* 129–134.

United States Department of Education. (1998). *Preventing bullying: A manual for schools and communities.* Los Angeles, CA: Author.

Vernon, A. (1993). *Counseling children and adolescents.* Denver, CO: Love.

Vernon, A. (1997). Applications of REBT with children and adolescents. In J. Yankura & W. Dryden (Eds.), *Special applications of REBT-A therapist's casebook* (pp. 11–33). New York: Springer Publishing Company.

Walker, H. M., Colvin, G., & Ramsey, E. (1995). *Antisocial behavior in school: Strategies and best practices.* Pacific Grove, CA: Brooks/Cole.

Walker, H. M., Horner, R. H., Sugai, G., Bullis, M., Spraque, J. R., Bricker, D., & Kaufman, M. J. (1996). Integrated approaches to preventing antisocial behavior patterns among school-age children and youth. *Journal of Emotional and Behavioral Disorders, 4,* 193–256.

Walker, H. M., Kavanagh, K., Stiller, B., Golly, A., Severson, H. H., & Feil, E. G. (1998). First step to success: An early intervention approach for preventing schools antisocial behavior. *Journal of Emotional and Behavioral Disorders, 6,* 66–80.

Walker, H. M., & Shinn, M. R. (2002). Structuring school-based interventions to achieve integrated primary, secondary, and tertiary preventions goals for safe and effective schools. In G. S. Stoner, M. R. Shinn, & H. M. Walker (Eds.), *Interventions for academic and behavior problems II: Preventative and remedial approaches* (pp. 1–25). Silver Spring, MD: National Association of School Psychologists.

Walker, H. M., Stiller, B., Golly, A., Kavanagh, K., Severson, H. H., & Feil, E. G. (1997). *First step to success: Helping young children overcome antisocial behavior.* Longmont, CO: Sopris West.

Waters, V. (1982). Therapies for children: Rational-emotive therapy. In C. R. Reynolds & T. B. Gutkin (Eds.), *Handbook of school psychology* (pp. 37–57). New York: John Wiley.

Wittmer, J. (1993). *Managing you school counseling program: K-12 developmental strategies.* Minneapolis, MN: Educational Media Corporation.

Zigler, E., Taussig, C., & Black, K. (1992). Early childhood intervention: A promising preventative for juvenile delinquency. *American Psychologist, 47,* 997–1006.

Chapter 4

PSYCHOPATHOLOGICAL AND PSYCHOSOCIAL FACTORS THAT CONTRIBUTE TO VIOLENT BEHAVIOR IN YOUTH

Patrice Paul

INTRODUCTION

Aggressive (violent) behaviors can take many different forms. Hostile aggression is marked by anger and has the primary goal of harming another person. Instrumental aggression is when harm to another is the means by which one can win some sort of competition or event. Regardless of their form, aggressive behaviors are one of the largest treatment issues in mental health (O'Donnell, 1985) and are associated with a wide range of psychological disturbances. There appears to be a heightened presence of psychopathology in violent youth (Knox, King, Hanna, Logan, & Ghazuiddin, 2000). This chapter will explore the relationship between aggression and various disorders of conduct (i.e., Conduct Disorder, Oppositional Defiant Disorder). A discussion of the comorbid presentation with cognitive (i.e., Attention-Deficit/Hyperactivity Disorder, Learning Disabilities) and emotional (i.e., Depression) factors will also be offered.

DISORDERS OF CONDUCT

Oppositional Defiant Disorder (ODD) and Conduct Disorder (CD) have been associated with aggressive (violent) behavior in youth. These disorders fall under the classification of externalizing disorders, and are the ones most likely to draw the attention of teachers and parents due to their disruptive nature. Unlike the criteria for depression (discussed later in this chapter), the diagnostic criteria are based on research with children and adolescents. The reader is directed to the latest edition of American Psychiatric Association, *Diagnostic and Statistical Manual of Mental Disorders.*

Oppositional Defiant Disorder and Conduct Disorder share a common theme of antisocial behaviors. Of the two, ODD is obviously the less severe, but there is significant evidence that if left unchecked these problems can progress into the more severe CD. There is considerable support that ODD and CD should be viewed as being on a continuum of severity with ODD being a precursor to CD (Hinshaw & Anderson, 1996). Several ideas support this conclusion. There is an earlier onset for ODD than for CD (Loeber, Green, Lahey, Christ, & Frick, 1992). Typically young children are diagnosed with ODD rather than CD. Children who move up in the continuum do not change behaviors but add more negative behaviors to their repertoire (Lahey & Loeber, 1994). The shift is from such behaviors as tantrums, irritability, defiance, and so on, to intermediate conduct problems (e.g., using weapons, lying, fighting, vandalism), to more advanced problems (e.g., mugging, cruelty, truancy, stealing). It is important to note that in the progression, boys who engage in physical fighting are more likely to transition to Conduct Disorder (Loeber, Green, Keenan, & Lahey, 1995). The progression of symptoms develops in a relatively sequential fashion (Loeber et al., 1995). In additional support of this developmental progression, the link with Antisocial Personality Disorder cannot be ignored. To meet diagnostic criteria as an adult, one must have been likely to be diagnosed with CD as a youth. As the spectrum suggests, the negative behaviors will continue to progress in severity and well into adulthood if not addressed early on.

Wakschlag and Keenan (2001) point out the importance of identifying these problems in early childhood. This is not an easy task, however, as many preschoolers exhibit difficult behaviors as a part of normal healthy development. In addition, problematic behaviors need to be differentiated from behaviors typical of a child with a difficult temperament. Children with difficult temperaments tend to have problems with transitional demands, and they tend to be irritable and difficult to soothe. Being able to distinguish between normative behaviors and those of clinical significance is important. As children grow and develop, these disruptive behaviors become all the more obvious and thus easier to diagnose as developmentally inappropriate.

There are many important characteristics demonstrated by youth with conduct problems that facilitate their aggressive behaviors. Individuals with these disorders have a set of cognitive biases that hinder the development and application of prosocial skills. These youth tend to believe aggressive acts are a legitimate form of action (Brendgen, Vitaro, Turgeon, & Poulin, 2002). They are more likely to assume that the victim "had it coming." They also lack empathy (Brendgen et al., 2002). It is difficult for them to take the perspective of another individual and internalize that experience in a meaningful way. Further, they distort the quality of their friendships and view them as positively as do adjusted children (Brendgen et al., 2002). Hence this misperception may lead them to further legitimize their negative behaviors. In addition, they tend to be hypervigilant to aggressive cues in others and the environment, to misinterpret the actions of others as being of hostile intent, to find their aggressive acts to be socially effective, and to be more suspicious of others' intent (Coie et al., 1999; Frick, 1998; Miller-Johnson, Coie, Maumary-Gremaud, Bierman, & the Conduct Problems Prevention Research Group, 2002; Zelli, Dodge, Laird, Lochman, & the Cognitive Problems Prevention Research Group, 1999).

It is important to note that not all children with ODD or CD are violent. Additional factors contribute to the presence of violent behavior. It is well documented that violence in youth is associated with dysfunctional patterns within the family and environment (e.g., Edwards, Barkley, Laneri, Fletcher, & Metevia, 2001; Loeber et al., 1995; Wakschlag & Keenan, 1995) that contribute to the diagnostic severity. Wakschlag and Keenan (2001) identify several factors that increase the likelihood of the development of disruptive behaviors in youth. Mothers in the authors' study who perceived themselves as experiencing strain within the parenting role were more likely to have children with these difficulties. Feeling that one's actions make little difference and that the child is a hindrance to the achievement of one's own goals may foster resentment toward the child. Isolation, low behavioral responsiveness, and the use of harsh discipline were also associated with behavior problems (Wakschlag & Keenan, 2001). Additional risk factors include parental substance use, inconsistent use of discipline, poor supervision, low socioeconomic status, and domestic violence (Lahey, Loeber, Quay, Frick, & Grimm, 1992; Loeber et al., 1995). Most of these concerns are present before the birth of the child and continue through his or her development. Wakschlag and

Keenan (2001) suggest that early identification of these risk factors is paramount in averting serious problems in the future. In their study of at-risk children who are between two and one-half years and five and one-half years old, the level of impairment was so pronounced that concern was raised that the preschool period may be too late to start prevention. Identifying these factors during the prenatal period might be the more effective time for planning prophylactic measures in averting the development of conduct problems in children who are at risk. These would include such things as the establishment of parental (e.g., psychotherapy) and environmental (e.g., access to employment, involvement in church groups) supports.

Many researchers (e.g., Coie et al., 1999; Miller-Johnson et al., 2002) note that peer relations are important factors in conduct problems. When looking at youth violence, the first relationship that most likely comes to mind is that of the bully and the victim. Salmivalli and Nieminen (2002) studied the differences between proactive and reactive aggression in youth identified as bullies, victims, and bully-victims. According to their findings, bullies and bully-victims are more likely to engage in reactive as well as proactive aggression. Victims are more likely to engage in reactive aggression, but at a lesser level than that of bullies and bully-victims. The relationship between bullies and victims is not the only source of aggression between children. Coie et al. (1999) found that among acquaintances, mutually aggressive dyads also account for a significant portion of youth violence. The authors emphasize the importance of assessing the relationship between two individuals as well as the internal factors each contributes to the dyad.

According to Miller-Johnson et al. (2002), both peer rejection and aggression in early school years are additional contributing factors to the development of conduct problems. Peer interactions and relationships provide a fertile ground for developing social skills. In the absence of those opportunities, the child does not have the opportunity to learn either through direct reinforcement (e.g., being included) or through modeling (e.g., watching/studying interactions). Of great concern is that these children may end up gravitating toward other deviant peers, further perpetuating their decline (Miller-Johnson et al., 2002). Sadly, the negative peer group provides reinforcement and modeling but for all the wrong behaviors. There is strong evidence that if these patterns establish themselves early in school-aged children, they will continue to be problematic as the child develops should steps not be taken to intervene (Miller-Johnson et al., 2002).

COMORBID COGNITIVE FACTORS

Attention-Deficit/Hyperactivity Disorder (ADHD)

The disruptive behaviors more commonly associated with the Hyperactive-Impulsive Type of ADHD are the focus of this section. A fairly substantial comorbidity exists between ADHD and Conduct Disorder/Oppositional Defiant Disorder (Shelton et al., 1998; Waschbusch et al., 2002). The comorbid presentation with ADHD is a predictor of violent behavior in youth with CD (Loeber et al., 1995). Children with ADHD and CD or ODD have higher reactions, behaviorally, physiologically, and emotionally, to peer provocation than children with ADHD or CD/ODD only (Waschbusch et al., 2002). These children with a comorbid presentation are more likely to offer an aggressive response to low provocation as well as to high provocation. It also takes those children longer to recover from a provocation.

The impulsive and disruptive features of ADHD are also important factors in the peer relatedness of these children. They are more likely to interrupt in play, disrupt the play of others, or have difficulty sustaining their attention long enough for appropriate play interactions. They will, therefore, be more likely to be rejected. "Because these rejected, aggressive children are more prone to anger themselves, as well as having fewer social skills for mediating peer distress, they may be more likely to get into escalating clashes with others, thus setting a pattern of greater interpersonal violence with peers" (Miller-Johnson et al., 2002, p. 227).

In addition, children with ADHD are more likely to be the victims of parental abuse due to the disruptive nature of their behaviors. These children are undoubtedly difficult to parent, particularly if the parent is experiencing additional internal (e.g., psychopathology) as well as external (e.g., loss of job) stresses. Abused children have a higher-than-expected rate of ADHD (Kaplan et al., 1998), and adolescents who were physically abused were more likely to face continued difficulties as related to the presence of ADHD (Cohen, Adler, Kaplan, Pelcovitz, & Mendel, 2002). Living in an abusive home also takes an emotional toll on these youth. Biederman, Faraone, and Lapey (1992) suggest that a substantial comorbidity exists between ADHD and depression.

Learning Disabilities

The comorbid presence of a learning disability can be an additional factor in the development of violent behavior in youth. Youth with learning disabilities are more likely than nondisabled peers to demonstrate violent behavior (Svetaz, Ireland, & Blum, 2000). Children with learning disorders tend to have social problems and to be devalued by their peers. This may be due, in part, to the impact of their specific processing deficit(s) on their ability to accurately interpret, problem-solve, and respond to their environment. For example, receptive and expressive language deficits are associated with social and behavioral maladjustment (Dery, Toupin, Pauze, Mercier, & Fortin, 1999; Vallance & Cummings, 1998). If one cannot find the words to express angry feelings, they will likely manifest in a negative behavior. As mentioned, learning-disabled children have deficits in their perceptual abilities (e.g., reading verbal and/or nonverbal cues). Nabuzoka and Smith (1999) found that younger children with learning disabilities have more difficulty distinguishing between serious and playful fighting. In their study, children with learning disabilities did not offer explanations or reasons for their judgments. The authors conclude that these children do not use as many environmental cues as compared to children without learning disabilities. Hence, they misinterpret their world, and with this information react inappropriately, furthering the likelihood of peer rejection and subsequent aggressive behavior.

COMORBID EMOTIONAL FACTORS: DEPRESSION

The word *depression* encompasses a wide range of behaviors and thoughts, and these descriptors often vary from individual to individual. Essentially, depressed individuals will present their sadness in their own idiosyncratic style. This poses a unique challenge for clinicians, especially when evaluating the presence of a mood disorder in a child or adolescent. Presently, the diagnosis of depression in youth is made with criteria more extensively studied in the adult population. For a diagnosis of Major Depression, there must be a major depressive episode that cannot be accounted for by any type of psychotic disorder, and there must not be a history of any manic episodes. Similarly, the diagnosis of Dysthymic Disorder—a low-grade, chronic depression—is based more so upon adult criteria.

Depression in youth manifests itself somewhat differently than that in an adult, and it overlaps significantly with other diagnostic criteria (Rehm & Sharp, 1996). Thus, one must be careful not to attribute some behaviors (e.g., aggression) as being related to a disorder of conduct when, in fact, it is suggestive of a depressed state. To that end, it is important to view depression from a developmental perspective. Wenar and Kerig (2000) and Wicks-Nelson and Israel (2003) offer a summary of the literature with respect to the specific age-related issues of depression throughout childhood. The expression of depression through childhood and adolescence has a close tie to the cognitive theories set forth by Jean Piaget (2000) and other cognitive theorists. As a child's cognitive capacities and language abilities mature, the expression of a depressed mood state will change and grow. Infants and preschoolers do not have the cognitive capacities to develop insight into their mood state. Their limited language abilities also preclude the exploration and expression of these feelings. School-aged children are functioning cognitively at a concrete level, and though they have a more expansive vocabulary, they also have a limited ability to make the connections between internal experiences and the outside world. Last, it takes time for an adolescent to fully develop the cognitive capabilities of full adult thinking (e.g., abstract reasoning). Thus, for these populations the expression of a depressed mood state is most likely to come through a behavior rather than through a conversation.

Of the symptoms listed in the adult criteria, irritability is one of the most significant features of depression in children and adolescents (Hammen & Rudolph, 1996). Irritability is closely connected with depression as well as aggressive behaviors. Research by Knox et al. (2000) found a high incidence of aggressive behaviors in depressed adolescents who were referred for treatment. There are several explanations regarding the connection between aggression and depression. Knox et al. (2000) suggest support from the frustration-aggression hypothesis (Berkowitz, 1989). In this theory, Berkowitz asserts that aggression is the result of an interaction between an internal emotional state and cues that are available in the environment. Frustration alone is not sufficient to produce aggression, but it creates a primer for an aggressive action. Whether aggression will occur can depend on many different factors (e.g., continued frustration, reinforcement for aggressive acts).

Frustration can also stem from the cognitive style of depressed individuals. It is not unusual for them to cognitively distort their world, and it is these distortions that may be a factor in aggressive behaviors seen in this population. Research indicates that cognitive biases in depressed individuals can include the following:

1. selective attention to negative information rather than positive information in the environment;
2. hypervigilance to negative cues in the environment;
3. externalization of successes and internalization of failures;
4. memory biases toward more negative events than positive events;
5. verbalization of more negative descriptors for events;
6. view that intentions from others are negative/hostile rather than positive/helpful;
7. rumination over negative events;
8. deficits/distortions in social cue detection;
9. negative conceptions of self and peers within relationships (Abramson, Seligman, & Teasdale, 1978; Nolen-Hoeksema, Girgus, & Seligman, 1992; Rudolph & Clark, 2001).

This cognitive style will lead to misperception of environmental cues (e.g., interpersonal interactions), and thus the focus on negative information can lead to a view that the world is a hostile and dangerous place. This can, in turn, lead to sadness, anger, and frustration, thus resulting in aggressive acts. As a result, the individual may view these acts as self-preserving and ultimately justifiable. Following this argument, he or she will be more likely to engage in those behaviors because they provide relief from the anger, removal of an unpleasant circumstance, and so forth.

It is also possible that the anger and frustration lead to feelings of helplessness and hopelessness. According to Abramson et al. (1978) depressed individuals attributional style leads them to feel helpless in the world. When a depressed person experiences a negative event or outcome, he or she will be prone to assume responsibility, and to assume that this does not change over time and across situations. Positive events will be externalized (e.g., rather than being proud of one's efforts at passing a test, the assumption will be that the instructor did not read the essay questions carefully and erred in one's favor). In this model, helpless thinking indicates a perceived inability to initiate positive change and escape the negative aspects of life (i.e., a failed escape response). Some individuals will, in response, "give up," while others may experience frustration that may result in aggression. Negative mood states will fuel that fire. Orobio de Castro, Slot, Bosch, Koops, and Veerman (2003) found that negative emotions lead aggressive youth to attribute the intent of others as hostile. This is a most notable problem for highly aggressive youth. To further complicate this issue, Trauting and Hinshaw (2001) found, aggressive boys with ADHD have lower self-esteem than those with nonaggressive ADHD.

Several studies have suggested that youth who are depressed, have poor parental attachments, or tend toward risk-taking behaviors are more likely to engage in aggressive behaviors (McCracken, Cantwell, & Hanna, 1993; Leas & Mellor, 2000), and they may be at an increased risk for future aggressive behavior problems (Schubiner, Scott, & Tzelepis, 1993). Although it may be thought that males would be prone to more physical aggression and females to more verbal aggression, research by Knox et al. (2000) suggests otherwise. In their study of clinically depressed adolescent males and females, they found that both genders were equally likely to engage in physical aggression. The authors hypothesize that this may reflect the increased observation of physical aggressive acts by females.

Environmental and family factors are important in the development of anger and frustration as it is related to depression and aggression. Research suggests that when youth are victimized or exposed to high levels of violence, both depression and aggression can occur (Goreman-Smith & Tolan, 1998; Knox et al., 2000; Singer, Anglin, Song, & Lunghofer, 1995). As stated above, an individual may become frustrated due to failed attempts to escape the adverse situation, be it living in a high-crime area or in a scenario of domestic violence or other abuse. Aggression may result as a last resort, so to speak, and an obviously unhealthy coping strategy, for an individual who feels powerless in an adverse situation.

Nonresponsive or overly punitive parenting styles can also lead to aggressive behaviors. The "absent" parent may fill the youth with feelings of abandonment. As a result, the child may aggress toward other people. Sadly, this will lead to continued rejection and, from a cognitive perspective, create a self-fulfilling prophecy that one is unworthy and unlovable. Overly punitive parents (the authoritarian style) are cold and place excessive and age-inappropriate demands on their children. The lack of warmth, coupled with harsh (and sometimes inconsistent) discipline, has been linked to depression and aggression (Baumrind, 1991). Silver, Field, Sanders, and Diego (2000) found that angry adolescents with higher levels of depression seemed to experience less intimacy with their parents and siblings, academic problems, and a greater likelihood of substance use. Parental psychopathology (e.g., anxiety, depression, substance use) is also an important factor in the development of a youth's agitated depression (Edwards et al., 2001).

Peer relationships are also an important factor in a child's psychosocial development, and aggressive behavior appears to be one of the largest factors linked to difficulties in peer relationships (Kupersmidt, Coie, & Dodge, 1990). Peer relationships can be viewed in terms of one's standing among classmates as well as the number and quality of dyadic friendships (Bukowski & Hoza, 1989). Research by Rudolph and Clark (2001) suggests that depressed children tend to believe that peers and friends are "untrustworthy and hostile" (p. 53). In turn, they view themselves as incompetent and unworthy. According to their findings, both aggressive children and those with co-occurring aggression/depression "experienced more severe social difficulties, including low rates of prosocial behavior and high rates of aggressive/disruptive behavior and alienation from the peer group" (p. 52). Being rejected and neglected by one's peers creates a substantial problem for these youth. Peers can serve as a helpful support resource during times of distress. These individuals, however, do not have access to that type of assistance and this, again, may substantiate a false belief system about the world and others.

TREATMENT FACTORS

Due to the complex diagnostic issues surrounding violent behavior in youth, a comprehensive assessment needs to be completed before embarking on any treatment plan or school-based intervention strategy. Such an assessment should be completed by a qualified professional, and it should include formal testing of both cognitive (e.g., intelligence, achievement, perceptual deficits, attention, memory, problem solving, language) as well as emotional functioning (e.g., depression) and environmental influences (e.g., domestic violence, child abuse). This is imperative because treatment must focus on the factors that are driving the violent/aggressive behaviors. Treating an attention problem with medication and classroom accommodations, and not the surrounding psychosocial (e.g., peer rejection) and family issues, would be an exercise in futility. For maximum effectiveness, the ideal scenario is that of a team of professionals both inside the school (e.g., school social worker, learning specialist) and outside the school (e.g., individual psychotherapist, family psychotherapist) working as a functional unit in the remediation of these problems. Parents may question why everyone must be, as it were, in the know about their child, but it must be explained that through such conversations between practitioners, there is greater continuity of care and subsequently better outcomes are reached.

There are many resources available in developing school-based programs directed at reducing violent and aggressive behaviors through social and emotional learning (SEL) and character education. The reader is encouraged to review materials available through the Collaborative for Academic, Social, and Emotional Learning (www.casel.org), which houses a comprehensive library of various SEL programs. Another helpful resource is *Promoting Social and Emotional Learning: Guidelines for Educators* (Elias et al., 1997). This book contains step-by-step instructions in completing a kind of needs assessment in the school, thereby affording the selection of the most appropriate SEL curriculum to meet the need of the students and community. Implementation and program evaluation strategies are also discussed. Regardless of the resource chosen, it is imperative that a properly trained team implements the program as outlined by the empirical research supporting the efficacy of the program. One must remember, however, that these programs are a supplement to the intense work done in the true therapeutic arena.

SUMMARY

The relationship between aggression and psychopathology is a complicated issue. A youth can have any combination of the aforementioned disorders, as well as be subjected to a variety of environmental and familial factors. Diagnostically, one must be careful about specifying the psychological origin of the problem so the appropriate treatment methods can be applied. In an ideal world, preventative measures as suggested by Wakschlag and Keenan (2001) could be put in place before the birth of the child, thereby eliminating or minimizing this problem before it has a chance to flourish. Unfortunately, our larger societal issues (e.g., limited prevention funding, economic uncertainties) preclude the implementation of such a plan at this time. As such, it is all the more important that parents, educators, and other care providers be aware of the diagnostic considerations and the specific presentation of aggression in youth so it can be targeted as early and efficiently as possible.

REFERENCES

Abramson, L. Y., Seligman, M. E. P., & Teasdale, J. (1978). Learned helplessness in humans: Critique and reformulation. *Journal of Abnormal Psychology, 87,* 49–74.

American Psychiatric Association. (2000). *Diagnostic and statistical manual of mental disorders* (4th ed., text rev.). Washington, DC: Author.

Baumrind, D. (1991). Parenting styles and adolescent development. In R. M. Lerner, A. C. Petersen, & J. Brooks-Gunn (Eds.), *Encyclopedia of adolescence.* New York: Garland.

Berkowitz, L. (1989). Frustration-aggression hypothesis: Examination and reformation. *Psychological Bulletin, 106,* 59–73.

Biederman, J., Faraone, S. V., & Lapey, K. (1992). Comorbidity of diagnosis in Attention-Deficit Hyperactivity Disorder. In G. Weiss (Ed.), *Child and adolescent psychiatric clinics of North America: Attention-Deficit Hyperactive Disorder* (pp. 335–360). Philadelphia: Sanders.

Brendgen, M., Vitaro, F., Turgeon, L., & Poulin, F. (2002). Assessing aggressive and depressed children's social relations with classmates and friends: A matter of perspective. *Journal of Abnormal Child Psychology, 30*(6), 609–624.

Bukowski, W. M., & Hoza, B. (1989). Popularity and friendship (issues in theory, measurement, and outcome). In T. J. Berndt & G. W. Ladd (Eds.), *Peer relationships in child development* (pp. 15–45). New York: Wiley.

Cohen, A. J., Adler, N., Kaplan, S. J., Pelcovitz, D., & Mandel, F. S. (2002). Interactional effects of marital status and physical abuse on adolescent psychopathology. *Child Abuse & Neglect, 26,* 277–288.

Coie, J. D., Dodge, K. A., Schwartz, D., Cillessen, A. H. N., Hubbard, J. A., Lemerise, E. A., & Bateman, H. (1999). It takes two to fight: A test of relational factors and a method for assessing aggressive dyads. *Developmental Psychology, 35,* 1179–1188.

Dery, M., Toupin, J., Pauze, R., Mercier, H., & Fortin, L. (1999). Neuropsychological characteristics of adolescents with Conduct Disorder: Association with attention-deficit-hyperactivity and aggression. *Journal of Abnormal Child Psychology, 27,* 225–236.

Edwards, G., Barkley, R. A., Laneri, M., Fletcher, K., & Metevia, L. (2001). Parent-adolescent conflict in teenagers with ADHD and ODD. *Journal of Abnormal Child Psychology, 29,* 557–572.

Elias, M., Zins, J. E., Weissberg, R. P., Frey, K. S., Greenberg, M. T., Haynes, N. M., Kessler, R., Schwab-Stone, M. E., & Shriver, T. P. (1997). *Promoting social and emotional learning: Guidelines for educators.* Alexandria, VA: Association for Supervision and Curriculum Development.

Frick, P. J. (1998). Conduct Disorder. In T. H. Ollendick & M. Hersen (Eds.), *Handbook of child psychopathology* (pp. 213–238). New York: Plenum Press.

Goreman-Smith, D., & Tolan, P. (1998). The role of exposure to community violence and developmental problems among inner-city youth. *Journal of the American Academy of Child and Adolescent Psychiatry, 36,* 1448–1456.

Hammen, C., & Rudolph, K. D. (1996). Childhood Depression. In E. J. Mash & R. A. Barkley (Eds.), *Child psychopathology* (pp. 153–195). New York: Guildford Press.

Hinshaw, S. P., & Anderson, C. A. (1996). Conduct and Oppositional Defiant Disorders. In E. J. Mash & R. A. Barkley (Eds.), *Child psychopathology* (pp. 113–149). New York: Guilford Press.

Kaplan, S. J., Pelcovitz, D., Salzinger, S., Weiner, M., Mandel, F. S., Lesser, M. L., & Labruna, V. E. (1998). Adolescent physical abuse: Risk for adolescent psychiatric disorders. *American Journal of Psychiatry, 155,* 954–959.

Knox, M., King, C., Hanna, G. L., Logan, D., & Ghazuiddin, N. (2000). Aggressive behavior in clinically depressed adolescents. *Journal of the American Academy of Child and Adolescent Psychiatry, 39*(5), 611–618.

Kupersmidt, J. B., Coie, J. D., & Dodge, K. A. (1990). The role of poor peer relationships in the development of disorder. In S. R. Asher & J. D. Coie (Eds.), *Peer rejection in childhood* (pp. 274–308). New York: Cambridge University Press.

Lahey, B. B., & Loeber, R. (1994). Framework for a developmental model of Oppositional Defiant Disorder and Conduct Disorder. In D. K. Routh (Ed.), *Disruptive behavior disorders in childhood* (pp. 139–180). New York: Plenum Press.

Lahey, B. B., Loeber, R., Quay, H. C., Frick, P. J., & Grimm, S. (1992). Oppositional Defiant and Conduct Disorders: Issues to be resolved for DSM-IV. *Journal of the American Academy of Child and Adolescent Psychiatry, 31,* 539–546.

Leas, L., & Mellor, D. (2000). Prediction of delinquency: The role of depression, risk-taking, and parental attachment. *Behaviour Change, 17,* 155–166.

Loeber, R., Green, S. M., Keenan, K., & Lahey, B. B. (1995). Which boys will fare worse? Early predictors of the onset of Conduct Disorder in a six-year longitudinal study. *Journal of the American Academy of Child and Adolescent Psychiatry, 34,* 499–509.

Loeber, R., Green, S. M., Lahey, B. B., Christ, M. A. G., & Frick, P. J. (1992). Developmental sequences in the age of onset of disruptive child behaviors. *Journal of Child and Family Studies, 1,* 21–41.

McCracken, J. T., Cantwell, D. P., & Hanna, G. L. (1993). Conduct Disorder and depression. In H. S. Koplewicz & E. Klass (Eds.), *Depression in children and adolescents* (pp. 121–132). Philadelphia: Harwood Academic Publishers.

Miller-Johnson, S., Coie, J. D., Maumary-Gremaud, A., Bierman, K., & the Conduct Problems Prevention Research Group. (2002). Peer rejection and aggression and early starter models of Conduct Disorder. *Journal of Abnormal Child Psychology, 30*(3), 217–230.

Nabuzoka, D., & Smith, P. K. (1999). Distinguishing serious and playful fighting by children with learning disabilities and nondisabled children. *Journal of Child Psychology and Psychiatry, 40,* 883–890.

Nolen-Hoeksema, S., Girgus, J. S., & Seligman, M. E. P. (1992). Predictors and consequences of depressed symptoms in children: A 5-year longitudinal study. *Journal of Abnormal Psychology, 101,* 405–422.

O'Donnell, D. J. (1985). Conduct disorders. In J. M. Weiner (Ed.), *Diagnosis and psychopharmacology of childhood and adolescent disorders.* New York: Wiley.

Orobio de Castro, B., Slot, N. W., Bosch, J. D., Koops, W., & Veerman, J. W. (2003). Negative feelings exacerbate hostile attributions of intent in highly aggressive boys. *Journal of Clinical Child and Adolescent Psychology, 32,* 56–65.

Piaget, J. (2000). Piaget's theory. In K. Lee (Ed.), *Childhood cognitive development: The essential readings. Essential readings in development psychology* (pp. 33–47). Malden, MA: Blackwell.

Rehm, L. P., & Sharp, R. N. (1996). Strategies from Childhood Depression. In M. A. Reinecke, F. M. Dattilio, & A. Freeman (Eds.), *Cognitive therapy with children and adolescents* (pp. 103–123). New York: Guilford Press.

Rudolph, K. D., & Clark, A. G. (2001). Conceptions of relationships in children with depressive and aggressive symptoms: Social-cognitive distortion or reality? *Journal of Abnormal Child Psychology, 29*(1), 41–56.

Salmivalli, C., & Nieminen, E. (2002). Proactive and reactive aggression among school bullies, victims, and bully-victims. *Aggressive Behavior, 28,* 30–34.

Schubiner, H., Scott, R., & Tzelepis, A. (1993). Exposure to violence among inner-city youth. *Journal of Adolescent Health, 14,* 214–219.

Shelton, T. L., Barkley, R. A., Crosswait, C., Moorehouse, M., Fletcher, K., Barrett, S., Jenkins, L., & Metevia, L. (1998). Psychiatric and psychological morbidity as a function of adaptive disability in preschool children with aggressive and hyperactive-impulsive-inattentive behavior. *Journal of Abnormal Child Psychology, 26,* 475–494.

Silver, M. E., Field, T. M., Sanders, C. E., & Diego, M. (2000). Angry adolescents who worry about becoming violent. *Adolescence, 35*(140), 663–669.

Singer, M. I., Anglin, T. V., Song, L., & Lunghofer, L. (1995). Adolescents' exposure to violence and associated symptoms of physical trauma. *Journal of the American Medical Association, 273,* 477–482.

Svetaz, M. V., Ireland, M., & Blum, R. (2000). Adolescents with learning disabilities: Risk and protective factors associated with emotional well-being: Findings from the National Longitudinal Study of Adolescent health. *Journal of Adolescent Health, 27,* 340–348.

Trauting, J. J., & Hinshaw, S. P. (2001). Depression and self-esteem in boys with Attention-Deficit/Hyperactivity Disorder: Associations with comorbid aggression and explanatory attributional mechanisms. *Journal of Abnormal Child Psychology, 29,* 23–39.

Vallance, D. D., & Cummings, R. L. (1998). Mediators of the risk for problem behavior in children with language learning disabilities. *Journal of Learning Disabilities, 31,* 160–171.

Wakschlag, L. S., & Keenan, K. (2001). Clinical significance and correlates of disruptive behavior in environmentally at-risk preschoolers. *Journal of Clinical Child Psychology, 30,* 262–275.

Waschbusch, D. A., Pelham, W. E., Jennings, J. R., Greiner, A. R., Tarter, R. E., & Moss, H. B. (2002). Reactive aggression in boys with disruptive behavior disorders: Behavior, physiology, and affect. *Journal of Abnormal Child Psychology, 30,* 641–656.

Wenar, C., & Kerig, P. (2000). *Developmental psychopathology* (4th ed.). Boston, MA: McGraw Hill.

Wicks-Nelson, R., & Israel, A. C. (2003). *Behavior disorders of childhood* (5th ed.). Upper Saddle River, NJ: Prentice Hall.

Zelli, A., Dodge, K. A., Laird, R. D., Lochman, J. E., & the Conduct Problems Prevention Research Group. (1999). The distinction between beliefs legitimizing aggression and deviant processing of social cues: Testing measurement validity and the hypothesis that biased processing mediates the effects of beliefs on aggression. *Journal of Personality and Social Psychology, 77,* 150–166.

Part II

ENACTING VIOLENCE PREVENTION PROGRAMMING

Chapter 5

THE TEACHING OF VIOLENCE PREVENTION IN A SCHOOL SETTING—WHAT CAN BE DONE?

Rene Pichler, Amanda Urban,
and Lynda Bockewitz

INTRODUCTION

Case Study

The school year begins and thousands of students return to the classroom to learn. As an educator, you find that several issues quickly come to your attention. You notice some students pushing, kicking, or even throwing things at each other in the halls and in the classroom. There is often yelling and even screaming among students and at various teachers. You have witnessed other students pushing desks across the room, along with their fellow classmates. One quickly becomes aware of the many factors present that could impede the learning process. Several concerns come to mind as you begin the school year. How will you capture their attention amidst the chaos? How can you ensure everyone's safety and manage to teach at the same time? How can any person function in such a chaotic and hostile environment? In what way can the devastating impact violence has in the school setting be affected by your role as an educator? What can be done to ensure a safe, comfortable, and productive learning environment for students?

Violence in the school setting has become a major concern in recent times. With the prevalence of recent school shootings and other violence at schools, a long-held and firm belief of most people that the school is a safe place has been challenged. Recent historical events have further led to concerns regarding safety in general and concerns about the safety and well-being of one's family. Media concerns and social agendas have driven the implementation of violence prevention programs, many of which have focused on the school environment as an effective way to reach many youth. Unfortunately, science has generally lagged behind in this area, and many programs are not well established in scientific theory nor are they evaluated as to their efficacy in a methodical, scientific manner.

One major caveat in the violence prevention literature is the lack of acceptance of a clear, concise, widely used definition of the phenomenon of youth violence. Criteria used to define the phenomenon of youth violence range widely from research project to research project. These definitions run the entire gamut from formal psychiatric diagnoses to simple acts of aggression as determined by reports from self and others. Other definitions use delinquency and criminal records as a measure. Still others define youth violence as only that act that results in institutionalization of the offending youth (Repucci, Woolard, & Fried, 1999). Leff, Power, Manz, Cosigan, and Nabors (2001) argue for defining aggression broadly in order to adequately encompass all forms of aggression, including daily gossiping, bullying, physical confrontation, and weapon use. This appears to be an argument substantiated by research, which indicates that violence escalates in a pattern from less aggressive to more aggressive behavior as well as the fact that there exists high comorbidity between relational and overt aggression.

Violence among school-age children and adolescents is generally defined as either overt or relational. Overt violence is most commonly employed by males and manifested through physical intimidation and outwardly aggressive behavior. Typically, this includes such activities as pushing, shoving, kicking, hitting, and punching. Overt violence typically increases in level of aggression over time and may lead to use of weapons or other forms of physical violence. Relational aggression is more commonly seen in females and generally involves manipulation of the relationship. Common behaviors observed in relational violence include such manifestations as gossiping, excluding persons from a peer group, or withdrawal of friendship (Leff et al., 2001).

Rates and incidents of violent crimes among youth are on the rise despite decreases in overall violent crimes in the United States. Juvenile homicide, aggravated assault, and robbery have surpassed adult rates in recent years, indicating that not only is juvenile crime on the rise but also that juvenile crime is manifesting in ever more violent ways (Repucci, Woolard, & Fried, 1999). Of further concern is the disproportionate numbers of ethnic minorities affected by violent crime. Reports indicate that African American youth have four times greater risk of being the victim of a homicide than Caucasian youth. Hispanics (three to four times greater risk) and Native Americans (two times greater risk) are also much more likely to be the victim of a homicide than their Caucasian counterparts. Overall, African American, Hispanic, and Native American youth are disproportionately represented in the statistics for assaultive violence (Botvin & Scheier, 1997).

Reports indicate that this violence is seen in all environments youth are exposed to; however, an alarming trend in the increase of violence in the schools has been noted in recent years. Many publicized school shootings are occurring throughout the nation with alarming frequency. Since 1992, there have been greater than 250 school deaths attributable to violent behavior. In addition, the United States ranks first among all industrialized nations in youth suicide and homicide rates. The statistics present a frightening trend in the violent behaviors of youth: 37 percent of high school students have been in a physical fight, and approximately 8 percent have been injured by a weapon at school. More alarming, 20 percent of youth admit to carrying a knife, gun, or other weapon regularly, 7 percent admitting to carrying a weapon on school property. Not only are youth becoming more violent, but more use violence as a form of conflict resolution. Also, these violent individuals are becoming emotionally detached from their behaviors (Clayton, Ballif-Spanvill, & Hunsaker, 2001). See chapter 4, "Psychopathological and Psychosocial Factors That Contribute to Violent Behavior in Youth" (Paul) for further discussion.

Preventing school violence is an ever more pressing issue and can be dealt with in a variety of ways. Many schools have implemented violence prevention programs in their curriculum either voluntarily or through legal mandate. There are more than 300 violence prevention programs available for implementation, and many include a structured intervention focusing on social skills acquisition, conflict resolution, and peer mediation. More common is the implementation of policies and procedures to deal with the issue of school violence. Many schools (more than 90%) have strict policies in place to deter school violence (i.e., so-called zero tolerance policies) as well as specific weapons policies regarding possession of a firearm or knife on school property. Further, many schools have implemented security measures ranging from locker searches to police presence (Howard, Flora, & Griffin, 1999).

TEACHING PROSOCIAL BEHAVIOR

Many people agree that preventing violence begins with respecting and learning to interact in an appropriate manner with others in the environment. For this reason, social skills instruction has come to the forefront in the discussion on ways to prevent school violence. Kamps and Kay (2002) report 60 social skills that should be acquired by elementary school students; they focus on classroom behavior, friendship-making skills, understanding and expressing feelings about oneself and others, alternative behaviors to aggression, and skills needed to deal with stress.

Controversy exists about whether prosocial behavior should be taught in the home or school environment. Parents of children who have learned appropriate social skills at home argue that valuable classroom instruction time should not be "wasted" on skills that the child should have already learned in the home environment. However, schools are faced with the growing problem in which children do not acquire the skills necessary to their social and academic success in the home environment. It is therefore considered essential that social skills be taught in the classroom, as those basic skills are a necessary foundation to acquire the academic skills that the school desires to impart. In addition, educators are well aware that disruptive behavior not only impacts the child but the entire learning community as well, making it essential that problem behaviors be controlled so that academic endeavors may be sought out.

Successful social skills programs employ various techniques to teach prosocial behavior and the acquisition of skills. Before choosing a program, the teachers and administration should evaluate several programs and make a decision based on the needs of their particular school. In teaching social skills, it is necessary to make sure several components are incorporated, including clearly defining the skill for students, modeling the skill, rehearsing the behavior with students, reviewing the skill, providing feedback on group and student performance, assigning homework, using incidental teaching and reinforcement throughout the day, and using contingency management and individual contracting as needed. Most important, the program chosen must be implemented in the entire school environment to be successful. All staff should be familiar with the program, and it should be consistent from the classroom to the lunchroom and playground settings. Additionally, parental involvement in maintaining the same language and contingencies in the home environment can be especially helpful for children with behavioral problems or a tendency toward antisocial behavior (Kamps & Kay, 2002).

VIOLENCE PREVENTION CURRICULUMS/PROGRAMS IN A SCHOOL SETTING

General Information

Research indicates that there are hundreds of violence prevention programs in existence. Granted, most do not have firm grounding in science or theories, but that has not stopped their proliferation and widespread use. The purpose of violence prevention is to reduce the numbers of juvenile perpetrators as well as juvenile victims of violent crime. In doing so, it is hoped that schools will function more efficaciously as the learning institutions they were designed to be. However, it is not until children feel safe that they can focus on learning and academic prowess.

According to Clayton et al. (2001), violence causes both physical and psychological damage to victims. Serious injury, psychiatric dysfunction, and even death can occur as a result. All of these consequences contribute to inability to learn, whether because of increased awareness and excitability; inattentiveness due to fear; or recurrent, intrusive thoughts of post-traumatic stress disorder. These problems are likely to arrest a child's development and lead to insecure attachments in relationships. Perpetrators, on the other hand, may develop deviant friendships, underachieve, or drop out of school, as well as continue the cycle of abuse. Moreover, socially rejected children are at a greater risk for later adjustment problems and are consistently found to be more aggressive and disruptive than children who are popular and average according to sociometric measures. Other negative consequences linked to childhood social deficiencies include learning difficulties (Amidon & Hoffman, 1965), dropping out of school, juvenile delinquency (Roff & Sells, 1968; Roff, Sells, & Golden, 1972), and psychiatric difficulties (Cowen, Pederson, Babijian, Izzo, & Trost, 1973; Pritchard & Graham, 1966; Watt, Stolorow, Lubensky, & McClelland, 1970). Moore (1967) described the phenomenon as a "snowball effect." Children exhibiting maladaptive behaviors are ignored or rejected by their peers, causing further aggression or withdrawal from social interaction. Furthermore, the social status of children becomes more stable with age, making it more difficult to modify (Coie & Dodge, 1983). This categorization follows through into the students' adulthood, making this phenomenon a lifelong process. Given the negative consequences that can occur, the need to institute effective violence prevention programs becomes even more apparent (Clayton et al., 2001).

Violence prevention programs are present in a variety of settings, including in schools, in community centers, and as part of religious organizations. By far the most common place to implement violence prevention programs is in the school setting, as it is seen as the most effective place to reach a large number of children. Depending on the program, it can be taught during class time or as part of an after-school program. Additionally, some programs focus on the school environment only, whereas others require parental, family, and community involvement.

Violence prevention programs run the gamut from kindergarten through high school age. Some schools focus only on younger children, while the most successful extend the same or similar programs throughout the academic environment. Specific types will be discussed in a later section. However, most programs have a large cognitive-behavioral component as well as a parenting component, especially in younger children. Most programs are designed to be instituted by teachers over the school years after training by behavioral specialists (Repucci et al., 1999). In other circumstances, the behavioral specialists may come into the classroom to teach the program, which gives the teacher time to prepare for the next lesson. If the violence prevention program is implemented after school, teachers may oversee the program along with other activity leaders to assist in monitoring behaviors.

Implementation and Development of Programs

Before a teaching professional selects a program, a number of factors should be considered. Clayton et al. (2001) suggest the following guidelines:

1. Programs should be founded on psychological, sociological, or educational theory.

2. Programs should be comprehensive, including promoting social norms against violence; should teach problem-solving and social skills; and should teach prosocial behavior in order to facilitate peace.
3. Programs should be appropriate for all children while taking into consideration unique populations.
4. Programs much ensure adequate teacher training in order for the program to be presented as intended and effectively.
5. Programs should strengthen children's self-worth and empower them to make appropriate and necessary changes.

In order to develop a program, one must first clearly delineate what it is that makes a school safe. Schools that are well run and function well to educate children share certain common goals. Algozzine (2002) recommends the following:

1. Strong academic and behavioral goals are in place, and school personnel are committed to carrying out these goals and helping students succeed.
2. Positive relationships are in place between students and school officials.
3. The school actively involves parents and the community at large.

Reaching these goals is not necessarily easy, but can be furthered in the following ways:

1. Possess attitude that all students can achieve academic success and behave in a socially responsible manner.
2. Make parents feel welcome at the school, address barriers to parental involvement, and positively engage families in education.
3. Develop strong links to the community through support services, community police, and faith-based communities.
4. Demand respect in the relationships between staff and students, along with trust, honesty, and openness.
5. Teach children about safety and consequences for behaviors that are inappropriate.
6. Have a system in place where students can feel safe reporting potential violence that they have knowledge of.
7. Provide a safe environment for students to express fears and concerns.

8. Have a referral system and protocol in place for child abuse victims.

9. Have before- and after-school programs that provide a wide range of activities.

10. Reinforce good citizenship in the school community.

11. Identify problems and monitor progress.

12. Provide support services to help students transition into adult life, for example, mentoring, internship, and apprenticeship programs.

Specific Examples

Clayton et al. (2001) present an excellent overview of violence prevention programs in their article, which will be reviewed briefly. The researchers reviewed 30 programs on the basis of goals, target skills, and theoretical constructs. These programs were categorized as antiviolence, conflict resolution, or peace programs. Antiviolence programs typically emphasize aggressive children's behavioral problems and cognitive-processing deficits. Programs typically employ instruction, cognitive-behavioral training, and the implementation of a reward/punishment paradigm. One example of an antiviolence program is BrainPower. This program specifically targets minority children, addressing cognitive-processing deficits, which often result in violent behavior. This is accomplished through small group activities pairing less skilled children with more skilled children and instructional training.

Conflict resolution programs consider violence to be an outcome of a lack of skills necessary to effectively deal with a situation without employing violence. These programs teach children to negotiate, communicate effectively, and allow for flexibility in dealing with conflicts through a repertoire of skills. An example of this type of program is the Interpersonal Cognitive Problem Solving (ICPS) program, which is also known as the I Can Problem Solve program. The goal of this program is to reduce early aggression, impulsivity, antisocial behavior, and other behaviors associated with lack of problem-solving ability. In ICPS training, three cognitive skills are targeted for skill acquisition: alternative thinking, consequential thinking, and means-end thinking.

Finally, peace programs were designed to incorporate both antiviolence and conflict resolution program ideals; they add, as well, the proactive idea of teaching children to relate to others in peaceful ways and respond to conflict in a creative ways. These programs attempt to teach resiliency to children, resulting in an enhanced sense of identity, a sense of purpose and future, a positive outlook on life, a sense of hopefulness, and the belief that life has meaning. An example of this type of program would be the Second Step Program, which is based on the theory that persons prone to violence are lacking in social skills, empathy, impulse control, problem-solving skills, and anger management skills. The program attempts to teach these skills as well as give children opportunities to practice the prosocial behaviors learned. There is a large parent component to the program accomplished through guides, meetings, and homework assignments. This component of the program allows families to learn the same skills as their children, which reinforces the use of newly acquired skills in other environments (Clayton et al., 2001).

EVALUATING THE PROGRAM

Program evaluation is a relatively neglected area in the violence prevention literature. Few programs employ adequate scientific measures of change, and even fewer examine anything other than immediate behavior changes. Long-term follow up is certainly a problem, as few longitudinal studies exist in this area. In order to determine the effectiveness of the program, evaluation should be incorporated into the program. Given the number of programs available, this type of evaluative information may be useful when selecting an appropriate program.

Positive Effects and Challenges

Throughout this chapter, it has been clear that there are several advantages to violence prevention programs. First of all, the skill-building component will enhance children's abilities to function and adapt to change throughout their lives. Considering the high cost of violence to society through not only the toll it takes on victims and perpetrators, but society as a whole, it seems necessary and beneficial to establish scientifically sound, effective programs. Second, after-school programs mentioned in this chapter would help to provide students with safe places to explore positive experiences. That alternative is certainly preferable to their being in unsafe communities unsupervised, which would lead to an increased likelihood of their involvement in violence. Finally, programs such as these are actually cost effective in the long run, presumably cutting down on the amount of money spent to house juveniles and adults in detention facilities, on court costs, on lost societal productivity during incarceration, and on victims' services.

Many argue that the programs are too costly to administer in large numbers. Although the initial investment may be high, long-term benefits clearly outweigh the initial investment. However, in a society where school curriculum cuts are more and more common, it may be difficult to justify the outlay of money for such a program when most parents want the school to teach only academic subjects. In the end, the question really is how much we value the future of peace in our society.

Practical Application of a Violence Prevention Program

This chapter is not only intended to educate individuals about violence prevention programs, but also to enable the application of this information in a realistic setting. If a formal program is not in place or cannot be feasibly implemented at the school, teachers and educators can make a conscious effort to incorporate these skills into their daily lessons plans. We understand that being a teacher requires a substantial amount of time and energy; however, preventing violence in youth should be viewed as an educational goal in our society. It is important not to feel alone during this process and to include your colleagues. Talk with administrators and fellow teachers about the importance of teaching violence prevention in the school, and provide suggestions on how to implement a program.

To implement a successful violence prevention program in your school, first identify the specific needs of the school. Some schools choose a targeted approach, focusing on those youth most at risk to engage in and/or be a victim of school violence; other programs focus on fostering a prosocial attitude in the entire school body through implementation of a comprehensive program. An example of a project in a Chicago-area school is contained in Appendix II. Once you have identified the needs of your particular school, research the available programs. Because many school violence programs exist, do not be overwhelmed by the sheer volume of material. Ideally, a program should be based on a scientific theory and have empirical data to support its use. Finally, choose the program that is most suitable for your school. Make use of resources that may be available to your school, such as school psychologists, social workers, parents, volunteers, the Internet, and books. Appendix I contains a representative listing of Web resources for violence prevention programming. The bibliography contains a listing of book resources for violence prevention programming.

By being active and implementing the most effective violence prevention program, you will begin to observe changes not only with your students but also with your fellow teachers. By implementing the program, the staff can model appropriate behaviors (i.e., social skills, conflict resolution, etc.) in the school setting and at home. This includes the classroom, hallway, and playground, as well as the family.

With many resources available for program implementation (see Corvo, 1997; Chaiken, 1998 in the bibliography), a more consistent school program can be conducted successfully.

REFERENCES

Algozzine, B. (2002). Building effective prevention practices. In Pam Kay, (Ed.), *Preventing problem behaviors: A handbook of successful prevention strategies* (pp. 220–234). Thousand Oaks, CA: Corwin Press.

Amidon, E.J., & Hoffman, C. (1965). Can teachers help the socially rejected? *Elementary School Journal, 66,* 149–154.

Botvin, G.J., & Scheier, L. M. (1997). Preventing drug abuse and violence. In D.K. Wilson, J.R. Rodrigue, & W.C. Taylor (Eds.), *Health-promoting and health-compromising behaviors among minority youth* (pp. 55–89). Washington, DC: APA Books.

Clayton, C.J., Ballif-Spanvill, B., & Hunsaker, M.D. (2001). Preventing violence and teaching peace: A review of promising and effective antiviolence conflict-resolution, and peace programs for elementary school children. *Applied & Preventative Psychology, 10*(1), 1–35.

Coie, J.D., & Dodge, K.A. (1983). Continuities and changes in children's social status: A five-year longitudinal study. *Merrill-Palmer Quarterly, 29*(3), 261–282.

Cowen, E.L., Pederson, A., Babijian, H., Izzo, L.D., & Trost, M.A. (1973). Long-term follow-up of early detected vulnerable children. *Journal of Consulting and Clinical Psychology, 111,* 438–446.

Howard, K.A., Flora, J., & Griffin, M. (1999). Violence-prevention programs in schools: State of the science and implications for future research. *Applied & Preventive Psychology, 8*(3), 197–215.

Kamps, D., & Kay, P. (2002). Preventing problems through social skills instruction, In R. Algozzine & P. Kay (Eds.), *What works: How schools can prevent behavior problems.* Thousand Oaks, CA: Corwin Press.

Leff, S.S., Power, T.J., Manz, P.H., Cosigan, T.E., & Nabors, L.A. (2001). School-based aggression prevention programs for young children: Current status and implications for violence prevention. *School Psychology Review, 30*(3), 344–362.

Moore, S. (1967). Correlates of peer acceptance in nursery school children. In W.W. Hartup & N.L. Smothergill (Eds.), *The young child: Reviews of research* (pp. 229–247). Washington, DC: National Association for the Education of Young Children.

Pritchard, M., & Graham, P. (1966). An investigation of a group of patients who have attended both the child and adult departments of the same psychiatric hospital. *British Journal of Psychiatry, 112,* 603–612.

Reppucci, N.D., Woolard, J.L., & Fried, C.S. (1999). Social, community, and preventive interventions. *Annual Review of Psychology, 50,* 387–418.

Roff, M., & Sells, S.B. (1968). Juvenile delinquency in relation to peer acceptance-rejection and sociometric status. *Psychology in the Schools, 5,* 3–18.

Roff, M., Sells, S.B., & Golden, M.M. (1972). *Social adjustment and personality development in children.* Minneapolis: University of Minnesota Press.

Watt, N.E., Stolorow, R.D., Lubensky, A.W., & McClelland, D.C. (1970). School adjustment and behavior of children hospitalized for schizophrenia as adults. *American Journal of Orthopsychiatry, 40,* 637–657.

Chapter 6

INDIVIDUALIZED THERAPY APPROACHES: VICTIM'S FOCUS

Theresa Risolo and Amy C. Patella

The private practice setting affords a unique opportunity to view the issues related to bullying and to intervening with children and adolescents who are the victims of this behavior. Individual psychotherapy with these clients is one arrow in the quiver. The private practice clinician has the opening to work with the individual child, the family unit, and the school environment. The unique chance to impact on a multidisciplinary level is clear when we listen to the voices of children and adults. These comments provide a context in this discussion about the victims of peer bullying:

> Oh, of course, our school district has a policy about bullying. Is it implemented—ha! The children are cruel. It happens every day, no one intervenes.
>
> —Parent of junior high female

> Others made fun of me; now they don't dare. I am the enforcer. I will beat them up.
>
> —Adolescent female

> I'd say "dude, leave him alone."
>
> —Adolescent male

> Our new principal has made this a top priority. He is on top of it. He is involving kids, parents, teachers. It [bullying] will not be tolerated.
>
> —Parent, middle school children

Over the past 25 years, the clinical community and the general public have become increasingly aware of the consequences of violence. The issues of domestic violence, child abuse, hate crimes, and aggression directed at specific groups are widely reported and commented on. The violence by students in Colorado, California, and Tennessee have forced schools and the mental health community to address a public health issue that, at its worst, has taken innocent lives. In its less dramatic outcomes, bullying has chronic lifetime implications for both the victims and the perpetrators.

Our attention was first directed to peer aggression and bullying in the late 1970s (Olweus, 1992). Seminal research was conducted by Olweus, and his observations provided insight into the complexity of children's behaviors. The magnitude of the observed problems led to clearer definitions of bullying and allowed other researchers to replicate Olweus's results (Nansel, Overpeck, Pilla, Ruan, Simons-Morton, & Scheidt, 2001). As a result of these studies, we have come to define bullying as a form of aggression in which an individual intends to harm another person; it is chronic in frequency and exists due to an imbalance in power. The disproportion of power may be due to physical size and age, or to psychological factors, such as a perceived group status and popularity.

The expressions of bullying behavior vary according to the age and sex of the children. When children are between the ages of six and nine years, the forms of bullying are more overt: physical confrontations, pushing, hitting, shoving, and stealing from the victims. These actions are more commonly directed by boys toward boys. Bullying also has less physical forms such as verbal taunts, harassment, and threats of exclusion (Bernstein & Watson, 1997). Girls tend to lead the way in verbal forms of bullying, utilizing name-calling, rumors, criticism with facial expression, and exclusion from interpersonal relationships (Nansel et al., 2001; Bendtro, 2001). In young grade-school–age children, the behaviors that define bullying may seem developmentally age appropriate, but the extenuating circumstances (e.g., differences in size or age) actually define the acts as abusive and violent.

In examining the phenomenon of bullying, cross-cultural studies indicate prevalence rates as low as 15 percent in some countries to as high as 70 percent in other countries (Haynie, Eitel, Crump, Saylor, Yu, & Simons-Morton, 2001). The World Health Organizational data surveyed for the United States in 1998 found that almost 30 percent of students surveyed identified involvement as a bully, victim, or both.

This data is the result of self-report accounts and indicates the broad impact of this behavior on students. What accounts for these different rates of prevalence? It appears that if cultural acceptance of aggression and aggressive behaviors is high and the modeling of alternative behaviors is low, if parental style is authoritarian and the social environment of the school is negligent in confronting bullying, all of these factors coalesce to allow greater incidences of bullying.

The effects of bullying manifest in a variety of ways, including absenteeism. The frequency of absenteeism is thought to be as high as 165,000 children per day in the United States. In 1999, the Department of Justice found that close to 1 million students, from ages 12 to 18 years, reported a fear of being harmed in school during the previous six-month period (American College of Preventative Medicine, 2002).

Research has shown that children who are victimized by bullies dread attending school, often creating "an internal map of unsafe zones such as bathrooms, the playground, and the route to the school" (Bendtro, 2001). The victim-child is often a loner, a child who feels both abandoned by peers and adults. This child is quiet, sensitive, and unable to repel the bully. This child often lacks close friends and is perceived to be a target of the bully because no one will try to protect this child or fend off the bully for fear of being targeted as well. What would appear to be indifference on the part of other children is often really a fear of being victimized themselves.

The child who identifies as a bully or bully/victim is characterized by a lack of empathy, aggressiveness, physical strength, impulsivity, and dislike of school (Haynie et al., 2001; Nansel et al., 2001). The child who engages in bullying is frequently a popular child, one who might even be described as grandiose in his or her self-perception (Fleming, Harachi, & Catalano, 2001).

Adults show a myriad of reactions when faced with the issue of peer victimization. Parents in particular react with a range of emotions. On some level, parents feel the pain their children are subjected to as victims. Some parents are forced to confront demons in their closets as their children's experiences dredge up their own memories of victimization by bullies. Parents also react with embarrassment. In *Odd Girl Out,* Simmons (2002) examined the phenomenon of alternative aggressions among school-aged girls. Alternate aggressive acts include social, relational, and indirect aggression—covert forms of bullying. Through interviews with Simmons, parents expressed both shock and shame when they learned their children were struggling socially. These parents felt as isolated and "different" as their victimized daughters. To confide in or to seek advice from other parents was to open themselves up to ridicule and judgment. There was a deep-seated fear that their children's victimization reflected poorly on their own parenting abilities (Simmons, 2002). These parents see themselves as failures. Indeed, parents who seek help from mental health professionals may also anticipate harsh criticism. These parents, who are suffering along with their children and are trying to improve a difficult situation, may feel as though they have been kicked while they were down by members of the mental health community. In Ambert's (1994) qualitative study, a man victimized in middle school reported that his psychiatrist blamed his parents for not being supportive enough.

While school is often the setting for much of the aggressive behavior that occurs among children, parents are cautious when reporting peer victimization to teachers and administrators. Specifically, parents fear that if they appear hysterical or overinvolved (Simmons, 2002), school personnel will dismiss their claims and their children will not be taken seriously.

At home, parents walk a fine line as they help their children navigate these social challenges. Some children displace their anger and frustration for the bullies who torment them onto their parents (Ambert, 1994). Expressing these volatile emotions to peers could lead to further physical abuse or social isolation. Children take out their pain on the people they believe would never desert them: their parents. Faced with their children's emotional ups and downs, parents may attempt to intervene in their children's social lives. They recommend that their children ignore certain classmates and befriend others. Although these interventions make logical sense, they fail to address the magical pull that some bullies possess. Several girls in Simmons (2002) book explained that they knew relationships with some friend-bullies were toxic, but they could not pull themselves away until the abuse was so severe, or the girls were so beaten down, that they could stand it no longer. The girls tolerated the bullies because they wanted acceptance.

Parents and other relatives may knowingly or unwittingly encourage aggressive behavior in youngsters. Morton (1997) found that parents of socially aggressive children tend to positively reinforce aggressive behavior while ignoring or punishing prosocial behavior. In neighborhoods where violence is common, and physical intimidation is deemed necessary to protect oneself, adults may encourage acts of aggression, especially when committed in retaliation for bullying. William, a fifth-grade boy at an inner-city elementary school, reported that his uncle punched him when he found out that William had walked away from a fight. His uncle said that he should always defend himself with physical force if he wanted to earn and maintain respect in his neighborhood. Many other children at William's school have reported that their parents or relatives recommend they use physical force when they are pushed, hit, or even called names by other children. This is consistent with Simmons's (2002) report that avoiding a fight or "staying hit" could lead to further victimization for some girls.

As noted earlier, many acts of peer victimization occur somewhere on school grounds. Twenty percent of students reported that they avoid the restrooms at school for fear of being victimized (Hanish & Guerra, 2000; Juvonea & Graham, 2001). Teachers and school officials are rightfully concerned about the prevalence of peer victimization, but it is often difficult for these adults to supervise every student interaction. Teachers hold so many responsibilities that it is nearly impossible to find the time to devote to the issue of bullying. Overworked teachers may recognize overt signs of bullying, such as fistfights between students, but alternative forms of aggression, such as spreading rumors, may go unnoticed and are, therefore, tacitly accepted (Simmons, 2002). Leff, Kupersmidt, and Patterson (1999) found that teachers correctly identified fewer than half of peer-reported class bullies and victims. If teachers cannot identify the socially aggressive children or their victims in a class, the burden to notify an adult is placed on the victim. Because many students doubt that teachers can have an effect on bullying (Roberts & Coursol, 1996), they suffer in silence.

Social aggression is difficult to identify in early adolescents. Elementary school teachers, who are with the same students all day, more accurately identified peer-reported bullies than did middle school teachers (Leff et al., 1999). With limited contact, it could be difficult for middle school teachers to see which of their students are socially aggressive. Also, by the middle school years, acts of bullying may be more covert and more difficult for teachers to spot (Leff et al., 1999). Ironically, just as social aggression is peaking, teachers are less able to identify the perpetrators and offer help to the victims (Cairns, Neckerman, & Cairns, 1989).

School administrators from across the country have taken steps to limit bullying in their schools, but this is a daunting task. School behavior codes usually forbid the use of physical force by and against students, but there are no rules when it comes to alternative, less overt aggression (Simmons, 2002). We must consider too that school rules often contradict rules of the street, and thus leave children confused as to how they should respond to acts of social aggression. Enforcement of school rules often depends on the victim's willingness to walk away from an incident of social aggression and notify an adult. This violates the code that many children live by outside of school: never lose face. Ironically, the very retaliatory act that will help them retain their dignity on the street can get them punished by administrators at school.

Application of school rules seems to dictate that these incidents be treated as discreet events. Administrators determine who acted first, then mete out appropriate punishments. This approach does not take into account the ongoing nature of peer victimization, wherein physical altercations are just one manifestation and conflicts between children can last for months or even years.

CHILDREN'S REACTIONS TO PEER VICTIMIZATION

It should come as no surprise that peer victimization can have deep and long-lasting effects on the victims. Children who suffer peer victimization tend to exhibit both personal problems (such as depression) and interpersonal problems. In a meta-analytic review of studies published between 1978 and 1997, Hawker and Boulton (2000) found evidence that victimization is associated with depression, loneliness, general anxiety, and low self-esteem. Victims tend to see themselves as socially incompetent and unaccepted by peers. They feel uncomfortable in social situations and report higher levels of social anxiety than do nonvictims. This is true of children of both sexes and all age levels who experience all types of peer aggression.

In their study on the effects of bullying among sixth-graders, Grills and Ollendick (2002) found that boys and girls with the highest rates of victimization tended to report higher levels of anxiety and lower levels of self-worth. It is not clear, however, if bullying causes these reactions in victimized children, or if these characteristics predate the bullying. According to Grills and Ollendick (2002), repeated victimization could lead to the development of anxiety and low self-worth among victims. The authors also suggest an alternative explanation: those children with high anxiety and low self-worth may exhibit some behavior or vulnerability that makes them targets for victimization. Their low sense of self-worth is then confirmed by their status as victim. A child's sense of self-worth seems to be key in buffering him or her from the negative effects of victimization. Boys with high levels of self-worth reported less anxiety than boys with low levels under similar conditions of peer victimization. Clinicians treating victims should consider this construct of self-worth when trying to increase their clients' resilience.

Children who are victimized report high levels of internalizing problems (Crick & Bigbee, 1998; Hodges & Perry, 1999). These children exhibit emotional distress, such as anxiety and sadness. They are quick to cry and tend to be socially withdrawn. They are known among peers to submit to their attackers' demands. These children are often rejected by their peers (Hodges & Perry, 1999). In their study of third- through seventh-graders, Hodges and Perry (1999) found that peer rejection and the presence of internalizing problems both predicted and resulted in peer victimization. Children who had internalizing problems and were rejected by their peers tended to be victims of direct physical abuse and verbal abuse. This victimization led to further increases in both peer rejection and the presence of internalizing problems. Children who are victimized may develop negative views of the world and themselves and show internalizing tendencies. These personal and interpersonal problems then make them vulnerable to further victimization (Crick & Bigbee, 1998).

Another consequence of victimization is reflected in the friendship choices victims make. Although victimization did not predict the number of friends a victim had, it did predict a change in the nature of the victim's friends. Children who had been victimized tended to befriend other children who were depressed, timid, and victimized (Hodges & Perry, 1999). This association with other victims may lead to further peer abuse. These children are less likely to stand up for each other in order to ward off aggressors. Aggressive children may prefer to attack peers who lack more supportive, socially adept friends because they can victimize without fear of retribution (Hodges & Perry, 1999). By helping victimized children build strong, healthy friendships and improve interpersonal interactions, the cycle of rejection and victimization may be interrupted. Crick and Bigbee (1998) suggest that victims of relational aggression in particular could benefit from learning to decrease internalizing behaviors and changing their reactions to peers in order to prevent future attacks.

Perceived deficits in children's abilities has also been linked to peer victimization. Among a group of multiethnic preadolescents in New York City, those students with negative communication beliefs and abilities reported more peer victimization, depression, loneliness, and social avoidance than those without these beliefs and abilities (Storch, Krain, Kovacs, & Barlas, 2002). These children perceived their communication abilities to be inadequate; they stuttered and had difficulty putting their thoughts into words. The researchers suggest that these communication difficulties provide a topic for aggressors, and because of their perceived or real communication deficits, the victims cannot verbally defend themselves (Storch et al., 2002). Like other bullying victims, they remain targets because the aggressors do not fear retaliation. It is likely that the bullying these children experience causes them to worry about peer evaluation. Rather than suffer humiliation at the hands of peers, they avoid social situations. As the researchers suggest, these children may avoid potential learning opportunities in their effort to avoid interacting socially with classmates (Storch et al., 2002). Those very children who could benefit from practicing verbal skills through social interaction deny themselves the opportunity for fear of further victimization.

When victimization is especially harsh, or victims are especially vulnerable, the results can be quite serious. Bond, Carlin, and Thomas (2001) reported in a study of Australian adolescents that a history of victimization predicted the onset of anxiety and depression, especially in girls. For some children and adolescents, the loneliness and helplessness of depression coupled with the desperation that results from chronic victimization may give rise to the use of violence against self or others among those affected. Cleary (2002) found that among a sample of adolescents in New York State, peer victimization was more common for students reporting suicidal and/or violent behavior compared to those reporting no such behavior. The risk of suicidal and/or violent behavior was 1.4 to 2.6 times greater among victimized students than among nonvictims.

Gender may play a role in the types of violent behavior exhibited by victims. Victimized females showed a greater frequency of suicidal, but not violent, behavior than their male counterparts. There were higher rates of nonsuicidal violence among male victims, as compared to female victims (Cleary, 2002). Although many adults view bullying as a typical childhood or adolescent pastime, this association between peer victimization and violence or suicide is alarming.

When children are victimized by peers, they develop coping strategies much like they would for any other type of problem. The type of coping strategy used and the gender of the child may contribute to the child's success in dealing with bullying. Kochenderfer-Ladd and Skinner (2002) found that among fourth-graders, boys who confronted peers and attempted to resolve peer arguments directly reported lower levels of loneliness and had fewer social problems. Boys who sought social support from peers outside the conflict, however, tended to be more lonely. The researchers suggest that peers may reward the boys who are direct with respect and friendship. Those seeking support from others are acting against gender expectations and may isolate themselves further.

Seeking social support does seem to be an effective strategy for victimized girls. Girls who turned to others for advice or help reduced their risk of social problems (Kochenderfer-Ladd & Skinner, 2002). Interestingly, however, girls who were not chronically victimized, but were merely bullied from time to time, developed more social problems when they sought social support. It is possible that the peer group does not recognize intermittent bullying as a problem requiring their concern and support. The researchers suggest that female peers may view these girls as especially needy or lacking in social skills.

Cognitive distancing, trying to put the problem out of one's head, was not particularly effective for boys or girls. Distancing was associated with greater anxiety for boys. This strategy may fail to work because the boys know that victimization can happen at any time and they cannot prevent it (Kochenderfer-Ladd & Skinner, 2002). Distancing was associated with greater loneliness and more social problems for girls as well. When girls ignore the problem instead of seeking the support of others, their concerns are not validated. Furthermore, if they use distancing instead of prevention, the victimization may just get worse.

Some children cope with victimization by internalizing the problem (blaming themselves) or by externalizing (taking their frustrations out on others) (Causey & Dubow, 1992). Externalizing was associated with greater loneliness for boys, perhaps because this isolates them from their peers and prevents them from having their concerns validated (Kochenderfer-Ladd & Skinner, 2002). Internalizing was associated with loneliness and anxious or depressive tendencies for boys. Internalizing and the associated anxious and depressive behaviors might make these boys reinforce their appearance as easy targets and they remain vulnerable to peer abuse (Kochenderfer-Ladd & Skinner, 2002).

It is clear that no one approach will work for every child. Gender plays a role (Kochenderfer-Ladd & Skinner, 2002), as do individual differences and environmental circumstances.

A hypothesis exists that bullying is created in an atmosphere in which there is a perceived imbalance of power, a lack of adult intervention, and a set of personal traits that link victim and bully. One must identify resources within each of these groups to provide interventions for the victims of bullying. The interventions directed toward the prevention of bullying must be multifaceted. The immediate behaviors of the bully must be stopped and the victim protected. The work in this dyad must be swift and decisive and nonpunitive to the bully. It is imperative that the interventions not replicate the behavior of the bully toward the bully. It is equally important for the victim to begin to take back the power given to the bully by being more assertive. The resources available to the child-victim are initially within the school confines. Therefore, engagement of relevant constituencies is critical to a successful program. The teachers, aides, school counselor, and administrators will provide the first line of intervention. Ideally, the school should have a well-developed policy and a procedure for managing these issues.

Within the school, the message must be one of respect due the individual, challenging stereotypes and fostering the acceptance of differences. The advent of so-called zero tolerance programs toward violence should not preclude the development of school communities that are nurturing, caring environments. The tendency to isolate and to marginalize the abuser does not systemically deal with the issues that cause and foster bullying. Without a systemic intervention, a new bully will rise to replace the exiled one.

In considering the actions that can take place within the classroom, several come to the fore. Teachers should observe and respond to teasing, pushing, and other behaviors that are consistent with the definition of bullying. A response directed to the bully that clearly communicates that the behavior is not acceptable is the first move. Providing a model for positively obtaining what he or she wants (attention and admiration) is the next step. As children vie for status within the group, they achieve prominence by bullying. A position of prominence and power allows the bully great discretion in how she or he relates to victims (Fleming et al., 2001; Hanish & Guerra, 2000).

The child who is the target must also be mentored. This child is encouraged to provide alternate response behaviors to being helpless. As simple as it may be, providing "lines" to kids helps. An example of this would be "name calling hurts, shoving is not allowed" (Bendtro, 2001; Bullock, 2002; Roberts & Coursol, 1996). With very young children, having a child from the upper grades as a shadow, so to speak, may provide the social and emotional support to engage in new, proactive behaviors.

Parental responses to a child who reports being bullied must be empathic and thoughtful. A child must be able to rely on the parental unit as both a source of succor and a source of strategies to cope with a bully. Care must be given to not minimize the impact of a bully's acts, and parents must probe carefully to uncover the extent of the behavior. For example, if a child reports that she or he is being snubbed, a parent should ascertain if this is in an isolated situation (i.e., time, place) or if it is pervasive throughout the day (lunch, recess, gym classes). The disruptions to a child's day impact her or his academic as well as social growth and must be addressed (Hanish & Guerra, 2000).

Parents must be willing to engage classroom teachers and other school personnel in challenging bullies. Younger children believe that adults can be helpful and do solicit help from adults. But by the time students reach high school, only 6 percent of the 66 percent of bullied students felt that school personnel assisted them in a meaningful way (Fleming et al., 2001). This perception of incompetence by adults must be challenged by specific, observable behavioral changes in the adults' behaviors.

The greatest opportunity for creating change over time is through intervention in the grade school years. Teachers and parents must recognize that there is a necessity for greater adult supervision in typically less structured parts of a child's day: lunch/recess, school bus, restrooms, and gym locker areas. Parents and teachers who respond directly, respectfully, and consistently by setting boundaries and alternative response behaviors garner the attention of youth and achieve a level of heightening safety within the school and between students (Roberts & Coursol, 1996; Smith, Shu, & Madsen, 2001). The nature of the coping skills and the social support provide children with the tools that allow them to avoid the role of victim.

Often, cultural norms regarding child discipline, personal defense, and acceptable social boundaries must be challenged and changed.

For example, the growing acceptance of so-called trash talk by athletes should be examined in light of verbal abuse that is used by bullies. Careful attention to the lyrics of rap performers gives insight into the paradigms that adults must challenge. A young teen accepts, without critical comment, the use of *nigger* and *bitch slap* because rappers use these terms with impunity. The casual acceptance of those degrading terms fosters a desensitization to the environment that allows bullying. Adults must engage children in thoughtful conversations about these images and stereotypes.

Child discipline that encourages and allows the demeaning of a child must also be challenged. How can adults expect children to refrain from hitting or bullying when this behavior is condoned within the home? How can a child solicit the protection of adults/parents when this same behavior occurs with the home? The psychologist in private practice must engage the school community and family in facing the issue of corporal punishment.

Precisely what are the skills that are lacking in a child who is bullied by others? Frequently this child has physical attributes that result in his or her being targeted. A child victim is often physically weaker and smaller than the bully. This child will often cry or give in to the demands of the bully. These qualities over time identify a child who will be victimized and revictimized. In therapy, we must assist the child in developing a verbal repertoire that allows her or him to respond with assertiveness.

A child who is victimized does not demonstrate the social skills that will deflect the aggressiveness of a bully. These children are frequently inept in coping with teasing, name-calling, or physical taunts. It is important to teach the child how to be verbally direct, to have body language that communicates confidence, and to be resilient in the face of abusive behaviors.

CONCLUSIONS

One hypothesis to explore is whether a continuum of behaviors that begins as peer bullying actually escalates to violent or homicidal acts. More research is needed to explore the correlation between bullying behavior, parental punishment, child abuse, domestic violence, and conduct disorders. It is reasonable to assume that behavior that began with peers and went unchallenged by adults and peers alike would be the preferred relational style into adulthood. In the business and professional community, this style is often rewarded and admired. One need only to browse the business section of the *Wall Street Journal* or *New York Times* to read profiles of corporate leaders who are praised for being tough and aggressive, or for bluntly challenging peers and subordinates. Is this lauded style nothing more but an accomplished, albeit more polished, form of bullying? Is it possible to think about the so-called problem behavior as one that desensitized the individual and the community to acts that are demeaning and aggressive? Does this desensitization set the stage for continued cycles of bullying that put all at risk?

The private practice psychologist must be prepared to use a multi-modal approach: parent-counseling sessions, school consultations, and individual work with the child. The child's therapy will focus on building a skill set of physical and verbal changes. The physical changes will include teaching the child to have good eye contact, good posture, and skills of self-presentation. The verbal skill set will include identifying feelings and behaviors, using direct verbal communications to fend off bullies and being assertive about one's needs.

REFERENCES

Ambert, A.M. (1994). An international perspective on parenting: Social change and social constructs. *Journal of Marriage and the Family, 56*(3), 529–543.

American College of Preventative Medicine. (2001). *Bullying behaviors among youth.* (Council on Scientific Affairs, Report XX, A-OZ): Author.

Bendtro, L.K. (2001). Worse than sticks and stones: Lessons from research on ridicule. *Reclaiming Children and Youth, 10*(1), 47–49, 53.

Bernstein, J.Y., & Watson, M.W. (1997). Children who are targets of bullying: A victim pattern. *Journal of Interpersonal Violence, 12,* 483–498.

Bond, L., Carlin, J.B., & Thomas, L. (2001). Does bullying cause emotional problems? A prospective study of young teenagers. *British Medical Journal, 323*(7311), 480–484.

Bullock, J. (2002, Spring). Bullying among children. *Childhood Education,* 130–133.

Cairns, R.B., Neckerman, H.S., & Cairns, B.D. (1989). Social networks and the shadows of synchrony. In G.R. Adams & R. Montemayor (Eds.), *Biology of adolescent behavior and development.* Thousand Oaks, CA: Sage.

Causey, D.L., & Dubow, E.F. (1992). Development of a self-report coping measure for elementary school children. *Journal of Clinical Child Psychology, 21*(1), 47–59.

Cleary, K.M. (2002). Risk factors for completed adolescent suicide: Implications for prevention. *Dissertation Abstracts International, 63*(03), 1557B.

Crick, N.R., & Bigbee, M.A. (1998). Relational and overt forms of peer victimization: A multiinformant approach. *Journal of Consulting and Clinical Psychology, 66*(2), 337–347.

Evans, W.P., Marte, P.M., & Betts, S. (2001). Adolescent suicide risk and peer-related violent behaviors and victimazation. *Journal of Interpersonal Violence, 16*(12), 1330–1348.

Fleming, C.B., Harachi, T.W., & Catalano, R.F. (2001). Assessing the effects of a school-based intervention on unscheduled school transfers during elementary school. *Evaluation Review, 25*(6), 655–679.

Hanish, L.D., & Guerra, N.G. (2000, December). Children who get victimized at school: What is known? What can be done? *Professional School Counseling,* 113–119.

Hawker, O.S.J., Boulton, M.J. (2000) Twenty years' research on peer victimization and psychosocial maladjustment: A meta-analytical review of cross-sectional studies. In *Annual progress in child psychiatry and child development 2000-2001.* New York: Brunner-Routledge. 505–534.

Haynie, D.L., Eitel, P., Crump, A.D., Saylor, K., Yu, K., & Simons-Morton, B. (2001). Bullies, victims, and bully-victims: Distinct groups of at-risk youth. *Journal of Early Adolescence, 21*(1), 29–49.

Hodges, E.V., & Perry, D.G. (1999). Personal and interpersonal antecedents and consequences of victimization by peers. *Journal of Personality and Social Psychology, 76*(4), 677–685.

Kochenderfer, B.J., & Ladd, G.W., (1996). Peer victimization: Manifestations and relations to school adjustment in kindergarten. *Journal of School Psychology, 34*(3), 267–283.

Kochenderfer-Ladd, B. & Skinner, K. (2002). Children's coping strategies: Moderators of the effects of peer victimization? *Developmental Psychology, 38*(2), 267–278.

Leff, S.S., Kupersmidt, J.B., & Patterson, C.J. (1999). Factors influencing teacher indentification of peer bullies and victims. *School Psychology Review, 28*(2), 505–517.

Morton, T.L. (1997). The relationship between parental locus of control and children's perception of control. *Journal of Genetic Psychology, 158*(2), 216–225.

Nansel, T.R., Overpeck, M., Pilla, R., Ruan, W.J., Simons-Morton, B., & Scheidt, P. (2001). Bullying behaviors among U.S. youth. *JAMA, 285*(16), 2094–2100.

Olweus, D. (1992). *Bullying at school: What we know and what we can do.* MA: Blackwell Publishers.

Roberts, W. B., & Coursol, D. H. (1996, February). Strategies for intervention with childhood and adolescent victims of bullying, teasing, and intimidation in school settings. *Elementary Guidance and Counseling* (30), 204–212.

Simmons, W. (2002). *Odd girl out: The hidden culture of aggression in girls.* New York: Harcourt.

Smith, P. K., Shu, S., & Madsen, K. (2001). Characteristics of victims of school bullying. In *Peer harassment in school* (pp. 332–351). New York: Guilford Press.

Storch, E. A., Krain, A. L., Kovacs, A. H. (2002). The relationship of communication beliefs and abilities to peer victimization in elementary school children. *Child Study Journal, 32*(4), 231–240.

U.S. Public Heath Service (1999). *Surgeon General's Call to Action to Prevent Suicide.* Washington, DC.

Chapter 7

BULLYING AND AGGRESSION AMONG YOUTH

James Galezewski

THE PHENOMENA OF BULLYING

Douglas Milteer died at 33, alone and destitute. Growing up, he was picked on by his two older brothers. He and his brothers were in fear of his mother's temper and violence—much of which was focused on Douglas. When he was in fifth grade, his parents divorced, and he moved in with his father. As well as moving from the East Coast to the West Coast, Douglas moved many other times, which would involve getting used to his father's girlfriends and their children. The Milteer boys became bullies—especially Douglas. They marked their turf by beating other, smaller students both in and out of class. When bullying others, Douglas was egged on by his brothers. As an adult, he bullied his coworkers and those who worked for him. He was known for his bad temper. His romantic relationships were short lived and marked by sexual infidelity.

After Douglas's death, his older brother told an old childhood friend, "We [the children] had no control at home, so we had to have control everywhere else. We controlled the bus. We controlled the bus stop. We controlled the baseball diamond. At gym, we controlled the red ball" (Eig, 2002).

Bullying is a growing phenomenon in the United States. Some 90 percent of middle school students have reported being bullied at some point in their time at school, beginning as early as preschool (Bernstein & Watson, 1997; Crick, Casas, & Ku, 1999; Egan &

Perry, 1998). The National Association of School Psychologists estimated in the late 1990s that in the United States, some 160,000
children miss school daily for fear of being bullied (Feldman, 1998;
Pollack, 1998).

This author defines *bullying* as aggressive behavior (usually chronic)
by a child or adolescent toward smaller and weaker peers for the purpose of gaining or regaining power and control, gaining emotional
gratification or eliminating emotional discomfort, or gaining peer status or acceptance. About 15 percent of students bully others at one
time or another.

A bully would not be a bully without a victim. Studies suggest that
child and adolescent bullies need a person or people to vent their
anger toward and to become the object of their aggression (Lorenz,
1966).

TYPES OF AGGRESSION

Researchers in child and adolescent violence have come up with
ways to break down and classify types of aggression in order to more
effectively treat it. In 1939, John Dollard published a foundational
monograph in which he stated that aggression was always a consequence of frustration, or the deliberate infliction of injury on a target
following the blocking of a desire or a perceived reward (Dollard,
Doob, Miller, Mowrer, & Sears, 1939). The generation of unpleasant
and uncomfortable feelings was added to the definition of frustration
by later researchers (Berkowitz, 1989; Rule, Taylor, & Dobbs, 1987;
Spielberg & Rutkin, 1974). This early definition has been narrowed
and refined over the years, and the terms *reactive* versus *proactive* and
overt versus *instrumental* are most commonly used when referring to
types of aggression.

Reactive aggression is defined as a type of aggression typified by so-
called hot-blooded anger, menacing hostile attacks, defensiveness in
response to a perceived threat, and intensive patterned autonomic
activation (physical agitation). This type of aggression is usually a frustration response, associated with a lack of self-control (Berkowitz,
1989; Dodge, Lochman, Harnish, Bates, & Pettit, 1997; Reis, 1974).
Reactive aggression includes facial displays of anger and rage, temper
tantrums, and vengeful hostility, whereas proactive aggression
includes bullying, domination, teasing, name-calling, and coercive
acts (Moyer, 1976; Price & Dodge, 1989).

Proactive (also called instrumental) aggression is highly organized, so-called cold-blooded, appetitive in nature, and characterized by little autonomic activation (i.e., physical agitation or excitement). This type of aggression is usually less emotional and is driven by the expectation of reward (Bandura, 1983; Moyer, 1976). Studies indicate that there is a significant trend toward increased proactive aggression among children and adolescents, a trend for which youth service providers are reportedly ill prepared (McAdams, 2002).

Reliable observations of these two types of aggression have also been made in young children's peer groups (Price & Dodge, 1989). In fact, these two types of aggression highly correlate respectively to diagnoses of Conduct Disorder (CD) and Attention-Deficit/Hyperactivity Disorder (ADHD), with reactive aggression found more in children with ADHD and proactive aggression more likely in those diagnosed with CD (Dodge et al., 1997).

There seems to be further classification of types of aggression according to the method of delivery of the anger. Overt aggression is behavior that involves direct verbal or physical aggression. In contrast, relational aggression is a behavior that is motivated with the intention to significantly manipulate or cause damage to another person's relationships or feeling of inclusion by the peer group.

BULLIES AND VICTIMS

About 15 percent of students bully others at one time or another. About half of bullies come from abusive homes. They tend to watch more television containing violence and misbehave more at school and home than nonbullies. When they get into trouble, bullies tend to blame others and try and lie their way out of consequences. They show little remorse for their actions (Garrity, Jens, & Porter, 1996; Kaltiala-Heino, Rimpela, Marttunen, Rimpela, & Rantanen, 1999).

Bullies and victims both use aggression as ways of coping with social and emotional discomfort. Recent studies found that both bullies and victims utilized both reactive and proactive aggression, while victims tended to only use reactive aggression (Camodeca, Goosens, Meerum Terwogt, & Schnengel, 2002). In short, victims tended to act out in frustration, possibly due to feelings of powerlessness and helplessness. Although bullies also tended to act out aggressively when feeling out of control, their aggression was also fueled at times by rewards, such as peer approval or bolstering their sense of self.

How does the experience of bullying impact the child who is the object of violence? How do the victims of bullying cope? The victims of bullies share several characteristics. Most often they are loners who are fairly passive. They tend to lack the social skills that might otherwise defuse a bully. Their coping styles tend to vary according to the type of aggression they experience and their age. In a recent study by Roecker Phelps (2001), it was found that child victims of bullying used more internalizing strategies, such taking the aggressive behaviors against them in silence or crying easily, for coping with relational aggression (such as peer rejection and social isolation), and that they used more externalizing strategies, such as returning violence with violence, for coping with overt verbal or physical aggression. Adolescent victims of bullying reported more use of externalizing and less use of internalizing strategies than did children. After a time of silently being the victim of bullying, the victim may snap, as it were, acting out in verbal aggression and physical violence. Profiles of such victims turned aggressive are described as having a low sense of self and as feeling unpopular and disconnected from their peers. These violent victims are described as finding identity and reconnection with others via violent retaliation (Pollack, 1998).

What causes bullying? To be more specific, what are the factors that cause a bully to develop? The answers may be found in looking at the development of the brain in children, at how patterns of thinking and feeling emerge, and at the impact of a child's social and family environment.

LIVING IN A VIOLENT WORLD

From birth, children exist in a world full of violence, and they are vulnerable to all its forms. Most children will be a witness to violence of one kind or another, especially through visual media, such as television, movies, and computer games, and through printed material, such as magazines.

Research evidence is clear that television, which contains so much violent content, has a great influence on the subsequent aggressive behavior of viewers (Huesmann, Moise, & Podolski, 1997; Sanson & diMuccio, 1993; Wood, Wong, & Chachere, 1991). In one longitudinal study, children's preferences for violent television shows at age 8 were related to the seriousness of criminal convictions by age 30 (Huesmann, 1986). Other evidence suggests that the observation of media violence can lead to a greater readiness to act aggressively and to insensitivity to the suffering of victims of aggression (Bushman & Geen, 1990; Gadow & Sprafkin, 1993; Linz, Donnerstein, & Penrod, 1988).

Many children and adolescents are exposed to actual violence from an early age. One survey conducted at a public hospital in a large urban area found that 1 in 10 children under that age of 6 reported witnessing a shooting or stabbing. Other studies suggest that one-third of children in some urban areas have seen a homicide and that two-thirds have seen a serious assault (Farver & Frosch, 1996; Groves, Groves, Zuckerman, Marans, & Cohen, 1993; Osofsky, 1997).

Some psychologists say that aggression is normal and natural. Pollack (1998) suggests that action (e.g., roughhousing and gentle teasing) is aggression that is developmentally appropriate and needs to be distinguished from violence. Yet, adults need to understand the difference between the two and keep children from crossing the line from action to violence.

BIOLOGICAL AND NEUROPSYCHOLOGICAL FOUNDATIONS OF AGGRESSION

Do bullying and aggression have a biological base? It has been suggested that indicators of aggression in later childhood and adolescence may be seen as early as in infancy. One possible source might be found in disruption of neural development. Neural development may be disrupted by maternal drug abuse, poor prenatal nutrition, or exposure to toxic agents (Needleman & Beringer, 1981; Rodning, Beckwith, & Howard, 1989). Even complications related to brain insult during delivery have been linked to later violence in longitudinal studies (Kandel & Mednick, 1991; Szatmari, Reitsma-Street, & Offord, 1986). After birth, brain development may be disrupted by deprivation of nutrition, stimulation, and even affection (Cravioto & Arrieta, 1983; Kraemer, 1988).

An infant's temperament or innate patterns of arousal and emotionality, which represent consistent and enduring characteristics and ways of responding to the environment, may lead in later life to violent ways of behaving in the face of stress. Inherent qualities, such as level of energy, evenness of mood, intensity of action, persistence, and distractibility, shape infants' responses to situations such as eating, sleeping, and playing (Carey, 1974; Kagan, 1984; Thomas & Chess,

1977). Infants with a so-called difficult temperament—irregular, avoidant, intense, and slow to adapt—may be less resilient to stress than those who have a temperament that allows for high levels of social responsiveness, autonomy, and flexibility (Thomas, Chess, & Birch, 1968). But not all children with a difficult temperament have problems. The key determinant seems to be the way parents respond to their infant's difficult behavior (Feldman, 1998).

Some theorists argue that aggression is an instinct, "hardwired" into the brain for the purposed of survival. Freud (1920) suggested in his psychoanalytic theory that humans have a death drive that leads them to take their inward hostility and strike out aggressively. Ethnologist Konrad Lorenz (1966, 1974) posited that humans share a fighting instinct connected to primitive drives to maintain territory and food and to weed out those who are weaker. Scientists who study the biological roots of social behavior (sociobiologists) argue that aggression promotes the survival of one's genes to pass on to future generations (McKenna, 1983; Reiss, 1984).

Preschoolers use aggression to attain desired goals, such as getting a toy away from another. Yet, in most children, aggression declines as children learn and use language to express their wishes and negotiate with others (Cummings, Iannoti, & Zahn-Waxler, 1989). Yet, aggression tends to be a stable characteristic. The most aggressive preschoolers tend to be the most aggressive children during the school-aged years (Ialongo, Vaden-Kiernan, & Kellam, 1998; Rosen, 1998; Kellam, Ling, Merisca, Brown, & Ialongo, 1998).

Studies suggest some interesting neurobiological factors in childhood aggression. In boys, testosterone levels have been positively correlated to irritability, impatience, and aggression (Olweus, Mattson, Schalling, & Low, 1988; Schaal, Tremblay, Soussignan, & Susman, 1996). A two-year study found a negative relationship between levels of the neurotransmitter serotonin and the severity of aggressive behavior (Kruesi, Hibbs, Zahn, & Keyser, 1992). Grayson (2002) studied physiological arousal patterns in response to film stimuli among children with behavioral difficulties. She found that aggressive boys had more response in the temporal lobes than nonaggressive boys.

There is also compelling evidence that children who bully and who may become antisocial tend to demonstrate neuropsychological deficits. Problems with *executive* (higher-order) functioning, such as those behaviors found in Attention-Deficit/Hyperactivity Disorder

(ADHD), may contribute to bullying. Children with ADHD tend to have deficits in the attentional and delay skills necessary to inhibit aggression and impulsivity (Dodge et al., 1997; Price, Daffner, Stowe, & Mesulam, 1990). Early speech and language problems (Beitchman, Hood, Rochon, & Peterson, 1989; Cohen, McDonald, Horodezky, & Davine, 1989), such as verbal mediation (or the ability to make one's self known and understood) and receptive listening and reading, lead to the development of behavioral difficulties. These skills are key factors in behavioral self-regulation, and acting-out behavior is negatively associated with a variety of relevant verbal skills (Hinshaw, 1992; Hogan & Quay, 1984). These deficits and aggression share variance that is independent of social class, race, test motivation, and academic attainment (Lynam, Moffit, & Stouthamer-Loebner, 1993; Moffitt, 1990).

Biological and neuropsychological factors, however, do not act independently of other factors, such as learned and developed patterns of thoughts and feelings and the social environment. Rather, they interact with it. For instance, even those children and adolescents who are at high risk for aggression due to biological or neuropsychological factors may be more likely to become bullies or act with chronic aggression if they live in a neglectful or conflict-ridden environment.

COGNITIVE/EMOTIONAL FOUNDATIONS OF AGGRESSION

In the midst of a baseball game, one adolescent boy slides into home plate, knocking down another boy. The boy who slid into home plate apologizes. The other boy begins to angrily push and shove, saying that it was done "on purpose." One boy interprets the event as an accident or even as part of the game. The other sees it as purposeful provocation and reacts aggressively. Some psychologists see aggression as a product of a child's or adolescents' social-information-processing patterns and attributions (interpretations of behavior) regarding the social interactions they encounter daily and of their own behavior. These information-processing patterns include the taking in of relevant verbal and nonverbal cues, interpretation of the social event as hostile or nonhostile, formulating aggressive or nonaggressive response options, and evaluating the response as desirable or not. Social-information-processing patterns act as proximal mechanisms for aggression, as deficits in these patterns are associated with a child or adolescent having a so-called hostile attributional bias, that is, being more prone to interpret benign actions as hostile ones (Dodge, Murphy, & Buchsbaum, 1984; Dodge & Newman, 1981).

Subsequently, in deciding how to respond to the intentions of another child or adolescent, a young person with a hostile attributional bias tends to respond with reactive, aggressive behavior on what he or she sees as a negative interpretation of another's behavior, although it may be an inaccurate interpretation (Dodge, 1991; Dodge & Crick, 1990; Dodge, Price, Bachorowski, & Newman, 1990; Nasby, Hayden, & dePaulo, 1979; Slaby & Guerra, 1988). Children who see others' behavior as aggressively motivated also tend to show less empathy, have trouble recognizing appropriate emotions in others, and have difficulty taking another person's perspective (Schonfeld, Schaffer, O'Connor, & Portnoy, 1988).

The way children or adolescents perceive and interpret the intentions of their peers also tend to drive how they evaluate outcomes (responses) to those intentions. Researchers found that aggressive children were more likely than their peers to choose aggressive strategies for solving problems and were more likely to evaluate those outcomes favorably (Crick & Ladd, 1990; Perry, Perry, & Rasmussen, 1986).

Hostile attributions and aggressive outcomes have a significant impact on the level of social acceptance a child or adolescent has. Studies suggest that the way in which children understand the causes of another child's behavior and how they anticipate and evaluate the outcomes of their social problem-solving strategies determine their level of social acceptance and the amount of successful social interaction they have (Crick & Ladd, 1990). Further studies (Dodge, Pettit, McClaskey, & Brown, 1986; Crick & Dodge, 1996; Dodge et al., 1990; Milich & Dodge, 1984; Slaby & Guerra, 1998) suggest that reactively and proactively aggressive children show deficits in social information processing, both in early and later stages, and, consequently, they experience problems relating to and being accepted by peers.

Research shows that *locus of control*, which is how someone perceives the cause of events, such as behavior and its consequences, has an impact on how one tends to act or react socially. On one end of the continuum, individuals with an external locus of control do not think they have much power or say in their lives. At the other end, youth with an internal locus of control believe that they are responsible for what happens to them (Strauss, 1994). Most bullies and, not surprisingly, victims have an external locus of control, possibly from chronically low self-esteem. This external locus of control may well lead to further perceptions of powerlessness and self-blame. This self-blame then, tends to be projected away from the self and toward the perceived cause of the problem or consequence. Whereas victims can point to the external source of their problems (the bullies), bullies tend to blame the victim.

Patterns of feeling as well as thinking come into play when examining the development of childhood aggression. Emotional factors include feelings of inadequacy, shame, and powerlessness, especially for males (Pollack, 1998).

Although the cognitive-affective approach to aggression does provide a way to understand the thinking and feeling processes that lead some children and adolescents to behave aggressively, it does not explain why inaccurate perceptions turn into violent behavior, or why aggressive children and adolescents assume that aggression is an appropriate response. Perhaps some of the answers might be found in examining family, peer, and societal influences on aggression.

SOCIAL/FAMILIAL FOUNDATIONS OF AGGRESSION

Albert Bandura (Bandura, 1983; Bandura, Ross, & Ross, 1963), a major proponent of Social Learning Theory, emphasizes that in contradiction to neurobiological explanations, aggression evolves from social and environmental influences. In short, aggression is a learned behavior, stemming from reinforcement from parents, other adults, and peers. Bandura has also hypothesized that exposure to aggressive role models (such as those in the child's family) is associated with the use of aggression, particularly if the observers are themselves angered, insulted, or frustrated.

AGGRESSION AND THE FAMILY

There are many family variables that go into whether a child is chronically aggressive or not and the intensity of that aggression. These variables go back to a child's infancy. If parents react to a child with a so-called difficult and demanding temperament by showing anger and inconsistency, then the child is more likely to experience behavior problems. On the other hand, parents who display warmth and consistency are more likely to have children who have fewer problems (Belsky, Fish, & Isabella, 1991; Teerikangas & Aronen, 1998).

Parenting style is a major variable in the development of a child's emotional structure and behavior. Children whose parents show uninvolved parenting styles tend to be dependent, moody, and hostile, showing lower levels of social skills and self-control (Baumrind, 1971, 1980). These findings are supported by data taken from the Child Development Project, a 14-year study of the development of conduct problems across childhood and adolescence, that suggested that parenting experiences (teaching behavior moderation, solving problems, methods of dealing with frustration and stress) are especially important in the first five years of life and have enduring effects on how a child manages her or his behavior (Feldman, 1998).

Dodge (1991) hypothesizes that early experiences of personal maltreatment and rejection by parents will lead a child to develop a tendency to display reactive violence. Child aggression is also correlated with marital discord, erratic and inconsistent use of punishment, and ineffective parental monitoring (Patterson, 1982) and with antisocial attitudes and substance abuse on the part of both the mother and father (Lahey et al., 1988; Lahey, Russo, Walker, & Piacentini, 1989). Physical aggression on the part of parents is known to be positively associated with how children regulate their emotions and adjust to social situations outside the home (Cohen & Brook, 1995; Eron & Heusmann, 1984; Martin & Clements, 2002).

Schulz's study (2002) suggests that the well-studied relationship of serotonin and aggression may have a familial dimension. He found that among a subgroup of clinically referred aggressive boys with lower serotonin (a neurotransmitter responsible for mood regulation), there was a higher incidence of aggression in the family.

Family structure and parental age also may affect the amount of aggression in children and adolescents. There are indicators that suggest that the younger the mother, the more problem behaviors a child is likely to demonstrate (Deijen, Blaauw, & Winkel, 2002). Having siblings may act as a buffer under high stress conditions (Lockwood, Gaylord, Kitzmann, & Cohen, 2002). This finding is important, as stress is associated with higher than normal levels of aggression.

Socioeconomic status (SES) may also have an impact on patterns of aggression in children and adolescents. Aggressive and Conduct-Disordered behavior is associated with family socioeconomic status

(Paternite, Loney, & Langhorne, 1976; Szatmari, Boyle, & Offord, 1989). The impact of poverty on the family tends to increase parental hostility and child-parent conflict (Paternite, Loney, & Langhorne, 1976).

PEER RELATIONSHIPS, REJECTION, AND AGGRESSION

As children develop, their understandings of who they are (self-concept) and how much they like themselves (self-esteem) shifts increasingly toward social comparison, or how they see others as seeing them. Self-concept and self-esteem become more differentiated as children mature, with such variables as academic performance, physical appearance, physical ability, and peer acceptance entering into the picture (Burnett, 1996; Marsh, 1990; Marsh & Holmes, 1990). If children see themselves as measuring up as compared to others, their sense of self grows. If a child or adolescent does not see himself or herself as keeping up with peers, his or her self-evaluation tends to become negative and is accompanied by a lowered self-concept and self-esteem.

Children and adolescents with chronically low self-concept and self-esteem have a tough road to follow, in part because their sense of self becomes a cycle of failure that becomes difficult to break. The child may experience consistent anxiety, frustration, and lack of effort, and she or he may begin to make downward social comparisons with others who are less liked and less competent (and weaker), as a way of psychologically protecting her or his sense of self. One tactic is getting into a crowd that is less socially proficient or less successful, especially if the child can dominate the group. In the child's mind's eye, it is better to be a big fish in a small pond than a small fish in a big pond (Feldman, 1998; Marsh & Parker, 1984).

Lack of popularity, which feeds into low self-esteem, bullying, and victimization, may take one of two forms (Asher & Rose, 1997). Neglected children and adolescents seem to receive little attention, either positive or negative, from their peers (Dubovitz, 1999). Rejected children and adolescents tend to be quite disliked, and they may get overtly negative feedback and treatment from their peers. Rejected children and adolescents tend to be disruptive, aggressive, uncooperative, short tempered, unfriendly, and dominating. In general, rejected youth lack social competence, and their behavior is seen as a problem by both peers and adults (Boivin, Dodge, & Coie, 1995; Volling, Mackinnon-Lewis, Rabiner, & Baraduran, 1993).

Yet, given his or her frustration levels and lack of social competence, a bully may use aggression, teasing, and violation of rules as a way to attempt to connect to peers or seek social approval (Pollack, 1998). However, a study of play groups of seven- to nine-year-old males found that reactive aggression and bullying were related to peer rejection (Coie, Dodge, & Kupersmidt, 1990; Coie, Dodge, Terry, & Wright, 1991). The more socially rejected boys in the study demonstrated a greater level of hostility toward others and tended to violate accepted rules when they showed aggressive behavior toward peers. Although bullying tactics may work, and bullies may be popular among their peers, some ironically find themselves victims of bullying (Olweus, 1993, 1995).

It needs to be noted that research conducted by Baumeister, Smart, and Bowden (1996) suggest that high self-esteem is often associated with violence and aggression. They found that perpetrators of violence frequently not only see themselves in a favorable light, but they in fact have an inflated view of themselves. According to this study, older children, adolescents, and adults with unusually high self-esteem are motivated to keep up their high level of self-regard and are motivated to use aggression when this view is challenged. This study suggests that programs that seek to raise self-esteem to levels that are incongruent with reality may not be the best approach for those who are aggressive.

GENDER DIFFERENCES

There are gender differences in how aggression is expressed. These differences seem to be based on learned behaviors and stereotypical societal expectations regarding the behavior of boys and girls. Studies suggest that from infancy, adults will play in a more so-to-speak rough and tumble way with males and will talk with them in ways that are more traditionally masculine (Jacklin, DiPietro, & Maccoby, 1984; Parke, 1996). Girls tend to gain status and emotional reinforcement through making friendship networks, being pleasant and friendly, having a nice physical appearance, being smart, and pleasing others. Boys, on the other hand, are admired for physical prowess and toughness, as well as intellectual ability, daring, and wit. Anger is accepted more from boys than from girls in both home and school settings. Hendrick and Stange (1991) found that in school, teachers are more likely to reinforce aggressive play in boys and criticize boys for traditionally cross-gender behaviors. In short, stereotypes tend to linger on in homes and schools, despite changing societal attitudes. These stereotypes apply to insult, ridicule, and bullying, as well as admiration and reward (Pollack, 1998). If boys or girls move away from gender-stereotyped behaviors, they are labeled tomboys or sissies. This socially conditioned training on how to express frustration and anger and to gain emotional reinforcement is a factor in the fact that boys are overwhelmingly more aggressive.

Possibly based on social conditioning, boys and girls show a marked divergence in the ways they demonstrate aggression and violence. Most violence is perpetrated by young males against males (Barrett, 1979; Camodeca et al., 2002). This fact has been held up in more recent studies, which found that males are more often both perpetrators and victims of overt and relational aggression (Suarez, 2002). Boys are more likely to anticipate negative self-evaluation and parental disapproval for acting aggressively, and boys are more likely to approve of aggression (Huesmann, Guerra, Zelli, & Miller, 1992; Perry, Perry, & Weiss, 1989). They are also more likely than girls to retaliate after being attacked (Darvill & Cheyne, 1981). Cross-culturally and historically, men have been the more violent sex (Gilligan, 1996).

There are many hypotheses as to why aggression and violence are more prominent among males. Beal (1994) writes that one of the motivations boys have to act aggressively is the blatant hierarchical social networks that they set up. This dominance hierarchy has an acknowledged leader, with members falling into different levels of status. Boys then learn to assertively or aggressively challenge and defend as they move up the hierarchy. Pollack (1998), writer of the popular book *Real Boys*, suggests that boys are taught that the only acceptable emotion is anger, which represents a disconnection from the full range of emotional expression. Violence, then, is an outcome of emotional disconnection. He further posits that there are socially taught "Boy Code" rules that call on boys to do everything possible to protect their honor and avoid shame, especially by going on the offensive, even if it means hurting someone. Jean Baker Miller, a researcher on men's and women's anger, has suggested that fear may be at the root of violent behavior in boys. This fear is related to boys' fragile sense of masculine identity (Miller, 1983).

In a study of preschool children's responses to problems, girls' problem-solving strategies were used more often and were more competent than those of boys, and they were less likely to involve retaliation or verbal and physical aggression (Roecker Phelps, 2001; Walker, Irving, & Berthelsen, 2002). The language used by girls is less confrontational and directive than that of boys, which is reflective of the tendency of girls to maintain equal status relationships rather than a dominance hierarchy (Beal, 1994; Goodwin, 1980, 1990). Yet, both males and females engage in increasing acts of verbal and physical aggression as they get older (Suarez, 2002). Yet, as males increase engaging in relational aggression, females decrease.

Gender differences in the expression of aggression is evident not only across socioeconomic groups in the United States, but across cultures, including Britain, Switzerland, Ethiopia, Kenya, India, the Philippines, Mexico, and Okinawa (Coie & Dodge, 1998; Whiting & Whiting, 1975).

INTERVENTION AND TREATMENT

Bullying is a real problem for children and adolescents, and without sustained intervention it will not go away. Many types of home-, school-, and therapy-based interventions have been designed to counter the bully phenomenon. Therapeutic interventions can provide significant and relatively lasting improvements for a range of child and adolescent problems, with a multisystemic approach working best (Strauss, 1994). These interventions focus on the way a child or adolescent feels (emotion), thinks (cognitions), and acts (behavior). More than 230 different treatment techniques are currently in use for children and adolescents (Kazdin, 1993).

Among individual therapy approaches, Perspective Taking, or knowing the cycle of violence, is a way of positively empowering the bully to think about violence and to respond in a different way. This form of cognitive-behavioral therapy consists of training the youth to identify triggers (such as events, people, and interactions) of their violence, what feelings (especially self-blame and discomfort) arise, and what thinking distortions power the violent reaction. Skill training in generating alternative ways to respond and in employing new and creative solutions to their problems is then taught. This type of therapy aids the bully in controlling the meaning of a situation and containing powerful disruptive emotions.

Garrison's and Stolberg's studies on the use of affective imagery (1983), found that this form of cognitive-behavioral treatment helped young people to identify and modify anger by focusing on the physical changes in their body and thoughts associated with prior emotional experiences. This treatment was effective in shifting away from angry-type feelings to those feelings more appropriate for the situation, with a decrease in aggressive behaviors.

Family therapy has proven useful for a range of child and adolescent problems and, compared to other types of therapy, has been shown to be more effective (Fishman, 1988; Goldenberg & Goldenberg, 1985). When family members are involved, changes are more likely to be maintained because the family system, with parents and siblings, and not just the individual bully or victim, is being transformed.

Parent training and education may help to reduce aggressive behavior and bullying. Pollack (1998) recommends that parents stay truly involved and connected with their children and notice what they are up to. Most important are what the parent does and how the parent behaves. He posits that parents are the primary models for such things as perspective taking and empathy, anger management, emotional expression, and behavior within relationships. According to Pollack (1998), forms of treatment that specializes in providing opportunities for parents to talk to their children and adolescents are paramount to prevention of aggression.

Many programs to stop bullying are school based and group focused, centering on primary prevention. These programs tend to address three different skill areas in which both bullies and victims usually have deficiencies: interpersonal skills, problem-solving skills, and cognitive-coping skills (Strauss, 1994). Some school-based programs deal with violence by what they call bully proofing. The students are trained about what behaviors make a bully and what behaviors make students attractive targets for bullies. Students then acquire skills in defusing situations in which bullies approach them. This program also attempts to redirect bully energy into positive activities, such as appointing them the "guardian" of victims (Pollack, 1998). Another popular program used in schools is the Second Step Program (Frey, Hirschstein, & Guzzo, 2001), which is a primary prevention program designed to deter aggression by promoting social competence in the areas of empathy, problem solving, and anger management. When unpopular children completed social competency programs, they tended to interact more with their peers, hold more conversations, develop higher self-esteem, and be more accepted by their peers (Asher & Rose, 1997; Bierman & Furman, 1984). Children in similar programs became more adept at accurately reading facial expressions, increased their sensitivity to others' emotions, and became better at making friends (Nowicki & Oxenford, 1989).

Carrity, Jens, and Porter (1996) suggest that victims of bullying can also be taught skills to help them cope and to decrease the possibility of their becoming aggressive. These skills may include leaving situations where bullying occurs, increasing their tolerance, understanding that they need not get upset by a bully's actions, and realizing that they are not to blame for the bully's behavior.

Although research had pointed to the fact that aggression can be controlled in many ways, it is unclear which interventions are the most effective. Personalities, circumstances, and environments vary, and their interactions are as individual as the children or adolescents.

REFERENCES

Asher, S. R., & Rose, A. J. (1997). Promoting children's social and emotional adjustment with peers. In P. Salovey & D. J. Sluyter (Eds.), *Emotional development and emotional intelligence: Educational implications* (pp. 196–230). New York: Basic Books.

Bandura, A. (1983). Psychological mechanisms of aggression. In R. Geen & E. Donnerstein (Eds.), *Aggression: Theoretical and empirical reviews: Vol. 1. Theoretical and methodological reviews* (pp. 1–40). New York: Academic Press.

Bandura, A., Ross, D., & Ross, S. (1963). Vicarious extinction of avoidance behavior. *Journal of Personality and Social Psychology, 49,* 521–532.

Barrett, D. E. (1979). A naturalistic study of sex differences in children's aggression. *Merrill-Palmer Quarterly, 23,* 193–203.

Baumeister, R. F., Smart, L., & Bowden, J. M. (1996). Relation of threatened egotism to violence and aggression: The dark side of high self-esteem. *Psychological Review, 103,* 5–33.

Baumrind, D. (1971). Current patterns of parental authority. *Developmental Psychology Monographs, 4*(1, pt. 2), pp. 1–103.

Baumrind, D. (1980). New directions in socialization research. *Psychological Bulletin, 35,* 638–652.

Beal, C. R. (1994). *Boys and girls: The development of gender roles.* New York: McGraw-Hill.

Beitchman, J. H., Hood, J., Rochon, J., & Peterson, M. (1989). Empirical classification of speech/language impairment in children: Vol. 2: Behavioral characteristics. *Journal of the American Academy of Child and Adolescent Psychiatry, 28,* 118–123.

Belsky, J., Fish, M., & Isabella, R. (1991). Continuity and discontinuity in infant negative and positive emotionality: Family antecedents and attachment consequences. *Developmental Psychology, 27,* 421–431.

Berkowitz, L. (1989). Frustration-aggression hypothesis: Examination and reformulation. *Psychological Bulletin, 106,* 59–73.

Bernstein, J.Y., & Watson, M.W. (1997). Children who are targets of bullying: A victim pattern. *Journal of Interpersonal Violence, 12,* 483–498.

Bierman, K.L., & Furman, W. (1984). The effects of social skills training and peer involvement on the social adjustment of preadolescents. *Child Development, 55,* 151–162.

Boivin, M., Dodge, K.A., & Coie, J.D. (1995). Individual-group behavioral similarity and peer status in experimental play groups of boys: The social misfit revisited. *Journal of Personality and Social Psychology, 69,* 269–279.

Burnett, P.C. (1996). Gender and grade differences in elementary school children's descriptive and evaluative self-statements and self-esteem. *School Psychology, 17,* 159–170.

Bushman, B.J., & Geen, R.G. (1990). Role of cognitive-emotional mediators and individual differences in the effects of media violence on aggression. *Journal of Personality and Social Psychology, 58,* 156–163.

Camodeca, M., Goosens, F.A., Meerum Terwogt, M., & Schnengel, C. (2002). Bullying and victimization among school-age children: Stability and links to proactive and reactive aggression. *Social Development, 11,* 332–345.

Carey, W.B. (1974). Nightwalking and temperament in infancy. *Journal of Pediatrics, 84,* 756–768.

Cohen, N.J., McDonald, J., Horodezky, N., & Davine, M. (1989). *Psychiatrically disturbed children with unsuspected language disorders: Psychiatric and language characteristics.* Paper presented at the annual meeting of the American Academy of Child and Adolescent Psychiatry, New York.

Coie, J.D., & Dodge, K.A. (1998). Aggression and antisocial behavior. In W. Damon & N. Eisenberg (Eds.), *Handbook of child psychology: Social, emotional and personal development* (Vol. 3, pp. 779–862). New York: John Wiley & Sons.

Coie, J.D., Dodge, K.A., & Kupersmidt, J. (1990). Group behavior and social status. In S.R. Asher & J.D. Coie (Eds.), *Peer rejection in childhood: Origins, consequences and intervention* (pp. 17–59). New York: Cambridge University Press.

Coie, J.D., Dodge, K.A., Terry, R., & Wright, V. (1991). The role of aggression in peer relations: An analysis of aggression episodes in boys play groups. *Child Development, 62,* 812–826.

Condry, J. (1989). *The psychology of television.* Hillsdale, NJ: Erlbaum.

Cravioto, J., & Arrieta, R. (1983). Malnutrition in childhood. In M. Rutter (Ed.), *Developmental neuropsychiatry* (pp. 32–51). New York: Guilford Press.

Crick, N. R., Casas, J. G., & Ku, H. (1999). Relational and physical forms of peer victimization in preschool. *Developmental Psychology, 35,* 376–385.

Crick, N. R., & Dodge, K. A. (1996). Social information-processing mechanisms in reactive and proactive aggression. *Child Development, 67,* 993–1002.

Crick, N. R., & Ladd, G. W. (1990). Children's perceptions of the outcomes of social strategies: Do the ends justify being mean? *Developmental Psychology, 26,* 612–620.

Cummings, E. M., Ianotti, R. J., & Zahn-Waxler, C. (1989). Aggression between peers in early childhood: Individual continuity and developmental change. *Child Development, 60,* 887–895.

Darvill, D., & Cheyne, J. A. (1981). *Sequential analysis of response to aggression: Age and sex effects.* Paper presented at the biennial meeting of the Society for Research in Child Development, Boston.

Deijen, J. B., Blaauw, E., & Winkel, F. W. (2002). Delinquency and aggression of school children in relation to maternal age. In R. R. Corrado (Ed.), *Multi-problem violent youth: A foundation for comparative research on needs, interventions and outcomes: Series I: Life and behavioral sciences,* (pp. 164–168). Amsterdam, Netherlands Antilles: IOS Press.

Dodge, K. A. (1991). The structure and function of reactive and proactive aggression. In D. J. Pepler & K. H. Rubin (Eds.), *The development and treatment of childhood aggression* (pp. 201–218). Hillsdale, NJ: Erlbaum.

Dodge, K. A., & Crick, N. R. (1990). Social information-processing bases of aggressive behavior in children. *Personality and Social Psychology Bulletin, 16,* 8–22.

Dodge, K. A., Lochman, J. E., Harnish, J. D., Bates, J. E., & Pettit, G. S. (1997). Reactive and proactive aggression in school children and psychiatrically impaired chronically assaultive youth. *Journal of Abnormal Psychology, 106,* 37–51.

Dodge, K. A., Murphy, R. R., & Buchsbaum, K. (1984). The assessment of intention-cue detection skills in children: Implications for developmental psychopathology. *Child Development, 55,* 163–173.

Dodge, K. A., & Newman, J. P. (1981). Biased decision-making processes in aggressive boys. *Journal of Abnormal Psychology, 90,* 375–379.

Dodge, K. A., Pettit, G. S., McClaskey, C. L. & Brown, M. (1986). Social competence in children. *Monographs of the Society for Research in Child Development, 44*(2, Serial No. 213).

Dodge, K. A., Price, J. M., Bachorowski, J., & Newman, J. M. (1990). Hostile attributional biases in severely aggressive adolescents. *Journal of Abnormal Psychology, 99,* 385–392.

Dollard, J., Doob, L., Miller, N., Mowrer, O., & Sears, R. (1939). *Frustration and aggression.* New Haven, CT: Yale University Press.

Dubowitz, H. (Ed.). (1999). *Neglected children: Research, practice and policy.* Newbury Park, CA: Sage Publications.

Egan, S. K., & Perry, D. G. (1998). Does low self-regard invite victimization? *Developmental Psychology, 34,* 299–309.

Eig, J. (2002, November 20). Violent, unhappy and brief: The life of a school bully. *The Wall Street Journal,* pp. A1, A8.

Eron, L. D., & Heusmann, L. R. (1984). The relation of prosocial behavior to the development of aggression and psychopathology. *Aggressive Behavior, 10,* 201–211.

Farver, J. A. M., & Frosch, D. L. (1996). L.A. stories: Aggression in preschoolers' spontaneous narratives after the riots of 1992. *Child Development, 67,* 19–32.

Feldman, R. S. (1998). *Child development.* Upper Saddle River, NJ: Prentice Hall.

Freud, S. (1920). *A general introduction to psychoanalysis.* New York: Boni & Liveright.

Frey, K. S., Hirschstein, M. K., & Guzzo, B. A. (2001). Second step: Preventing aggression by promoting social competence. In H. M. Walker & M. H. Epstein (Eds.), *Making schools safer and violence free: Critical issues, solutions and recommended practices* (pp. 88–98). Austin, TX: Pro-Ed.

Gadow, K. D., & Sprafkin, J. (1993). Television "violence" and children with emotional and behavioral disorders. *Journal of Emotional and Behavioral Disorders, 1,* 54–63.

Garrison, S. R., & Stolberg, A. L. (1983). Modification of anger in children by affective imagery training. *Journal of Abnormal Psychology, 11,* 115–129.

Garrity, C., Jens, K., & Porter, W. W. (1996). *Bully-victim problems in the school setting.* Paper presented at the annual meeting of the American Psychological Association. Toronto, Canada.

Gilligan, J. (1996). *Violence: Our deadly epidemic and its causes.* New York: Putnam.

Goodwin, M. H. (1980). Directive-response speech sequences in girls' and boys' task activities. In S. McConnell-Ginet, R. Borker, & N. Furman (Eds.), *Women and language in literature and society* (pp. 157–173). New York: Praeger.

Goodwin, M. H. (1990). Tactical uses of stories: Participation frameworks within girls' and boys' disputes. *Discourse Processes, 13,* 33–71.

Grayson, R. H. (2002). Physiological responsivity in aggressive and non-aggressive pre-pubertal children. *Dissertation Abstracts International: Section B: the Sciences and Engineering 62,* 5963.

Groves, B., Zuckerman, B., Marans, S., & Cohen, D. (1993). Silent victims: Children who witness violence. *Journal of the American Medical Association, 269,* 262–264.

Hendrick, J., & Stange, T. (1991). Do actions speak louder than words? An effect of the functional use of language on dominant sex role behavior in boys and girls. *Early Childhood Research Quarterly, 6,* 565–576.

Hinshaw, S. P. (1992). Externalizing behavior problems and academic under-achievement in childhood and adolescence: Causal relationships and underlying mechanisms. *Psychological Bulletin, 111,* 127–155.

Hogan, A. E., & Quay, H. C. (1984). Cognition in child and adolescent behaviors. In B. B. Lahey & A. E. Kazdin (Eds.), *Advances in clinical child psychology* (Vol. 7, pp. 1–34). New York: Plenum Press.

Huesmann, L. R. (1986). Psychological processes promoting the relations between exposure to media violence and aggressive behavior by the viewer. *Journal of Social Issues, 42,* 125–139.

Huesmann, L. R., Guerra, N. G., Zelli, A., & Miller, L. (1992). Differing normative beliefs about aggression for boys and girls. In K. Bjorkquist & P. Niemele (Eds.), *Of mice and women: Aspects of female aggression.* Orlando, FL: Academic Press.

Huesmann, L. R., Moise, J. F., & Podolski, C. (1997). The effects of media violence on the development of antisocial behavior. In D. M. Stoff, J. Brieling, & J. D. Maser (Eds.), *Handbook of antisocial behavior* (pp. 181–193). New York: John Wiley & Sons.

Ialongo, N. S., Vaden-Kiernan, N., & Kellam, S. (1998). Early peer rejection and aggression: Longitudinal relations with adolescent behavior. *Journal of Developmental & Physical Disabilities, 10,* 199–213.

Kagan, J. (1984). *The nature of the child.* New York: Basic Books.

Kaltiala-Heino, R., Rimpela, M., Marttunen, M., Rimpela, A., & Rantanen, P. (1999). Bullying, depression and suicidal ideation in Finnish adolescents: School survey. *British Medical Journal, 329,* 348–351.

Kandel, E., & Mednick, S. A. (1991). Perinatal complications predict violent offending. *Acta Psychiatrica Scandanavica, 78,* 1–5.

Kazdin, A. E. (1993). Adolescent mental health: Prevention and treatment. *American Psychologist, 48,* 127–141.

Kellam, S. G., Ling, X., Merisca, R., Brown, C. H., & Ialongo, N. (1998). The effect of the level of aggression on the course and malleability of aggressive behavior into middle school. *Development & Psychopathology, 10,* 165–185.

Kraemer, G. W. (1988). Speculations on the developmental neurobiology of protest and despair. In P. Simon, P. Soubrie, & D. Widlocher (Eds.), *Inquiry into schizophrenia and depression: Animal models of psychiatric disorders* (pp. 101–147). Basel, Switzerland: Karger.

Kruesi, M. J., Hibbs, E. D., Zahn, T. P., & Keyser, C. S. (1992). A 2-year prospective follow-up study of children and adolescents with disruptive behavior disorders: Prediction by cerebrospinal fluid 5-hydroxyindoleacetic acid, homovanillic acid and autonomic measures? *Archives of General Psychiatry, 49,* 429–435.

Lahey, B. B., Piacentini, J. C., McBurnett, K., Stone, P., Hartdagen, S., & Hynd, G. (1988). Psychopathology in the parents of children with Conduct Disorder and hyperactivity. *Journal of the American Academy of Child and Adolescent Psychiatry, 27,* 163–170.

Lahey, B. B., Russo, M. F., Walker, J. L., & Piacentini, J. C. (1989). Personality characteristics of the mothers of children with disruptive behavior disorders. *Journal of Consulting and Clinical Psychology, 57,* 512–515.

Linz, D. G., Donnerstein, E., & Penrod, S. (1988). Effects of long-term exposure to violent and sexually degrading depictions of women. *Journal of Personality and Social Psychology, 55,* 758–768.

Lockwood, R. L., Gaylord, P. K., Kitzmann, K. M., & Cohen, R. (2002). Family stress and children's rejection by peers: Do siblings provide a buffer? *Journal of Child and Family Studies, 11,* 331–345.

Lorenz, K. (1966). *On aggression.* New York: Harcourt, Brace, Jovanovich.

Lorenz, K. (1974). *Evolution and the modification of behavior.* Chicago: University of Chicago Press.

Lynam, D., Moffitt, T., & Stouthamer-Loeber, M. (1993). Explaining the relation between IQ and delinquency: Class, race, test motivation, school failure or self-control? *Journal of Abnormal Psychology, 102,* 187–196.

Marsh, H. W. (1990). Influences of internal and external frames of reference on the formation of math and English self-concepts. *Journal of Educational Psychology, 82,* 107–116.

Marsh, H. W., & Holmes, I. W. M. (1990). Multidimensional self-concepts: Construct validation of responses by children. *American Educational Research Journal, 27,* 89–118.

Marsh, H. W., & Parker, J. W. (1984). Determinants of student self-concept: Is it better to be a relatively big fish in a small pond even if you don't learn to swim as well? *Journal of Personality and Social Psychology, 47,* 89–118.

Martin, S. E., & Clements, S. L. (2002). Young children's responding to interparental conflict: Associates with marital aggression and child adjustment. *Journal of Child and Family Studies, 11,* 231–244.

McAdams, C. R. (2002). Trends in the occurrence of reactive and proactive aggression among children and adolescents: Implications for preparation and practice in child and youth care. *Child and Youth Care Forum, 31,* 89–109.

McKenna, J.J. (1983). Primate aggression and evolution: An overview of sociobiological and anthropological perspectives. *Bulletin of the American Academy of Psychiatry and the Law, 11,* 105–130.

Milich, R., & Dodge, K.A. (1984). Social information processing in child psychiatry populations. *Journal of Abnormal Child Psychology, 12,* 471–489.

Miller, J.B. (1983). *The construction of anger in women and men* (Stone Center Working Paper Series, work in progress No. 4). Wellesley, MA: Wellesley College, Stone Center.

Moffitt, T.E. (1990). The neuropsychology of delinquency: A critical review of theory and research. In N. Morris & M. Tonry (Eds.), *Crime and justice* (Vol. 12, pp. 99–169). Chicago: University of Chicago Press.

Moyer, K.E. (1976). *The psychobiology of aggression.* New York: Harper and Row.

Nasby, W., Hayden, B., & dePaulo, B.M. (1979). Attributional bias among aggressive boys to interpret unambiguous social stimuli as displays of hostility. *Journal of Abnormal Psychology, 89,* 459–468.

Needleman, H.L., & Beringer, D.C. (1981). The epidemiology of low-level lead exposure in childhood. *Journal of Child Psychiatry, 20,* 496–512.

Nowicki, S., & Oxenford, C. (1989). The relation of hostile nonverbal communication styles to popularity in preadolescent children. *Journal of Genetic Psychology, 150,* 39–44.

Olweus, D. (1993). *Bullying at school: What we know and what we can do.* Oxford, England: Blackwell.

Olweus, D. (1995). Bullying or peer abuse at school: Facts and intervention. *Current Directions in Psychological Science, 4,* 196–200.

Olweus, D., Mattson, A., Schalling, D., & Low, H. (1988). Circulating testosterone levels and aggression in adolescent males: A causal analysis. *Psychosomatic Medicine, 50,* 261–272.

Osofsky, J.D. (1997). The effects of exposure to violence on young children. *American Psychologist, 50,* 782–788.

Paternite, C.E., Loney, J., & Langhorne, J.E. (1976). Relationships between symptomatology and SES-related factors in hyperkinetic/MBD boys. *American Journal of Orthopsychiatry, 46,* 291–301.

Patterson, G.R., (1982). *Coercive family processes.* Eugene, OR: Castalia.

Perry, D.G., Perry, L.C., & Rasmussen, P. (1986). Cognitive social learning mediators of aggression. *Child Development, 57,* 700–711.

Perry, D.G., Perry, L.C., & Weiss, R.J. (1989). Sex differences in the consequences children anticipate for aggression. *Developmental Psychology, 25,* 312–320.

Pollack, W. (1998). *Real boys.* New York: Henry Holt and Company.

Price, B.H., Daffner, K.R., Stowe, R.M., & Mesulam, M.M. (1990). The comportmental learning disabilities of early frontal lobe damage. *Brain, 113,* 1383–1393.

Price, J.M., & Dodge, K.A. (1989). Reactive and proactive aggression in childhood: Relations to peer status and social context dimensions. *Journal of Abnormal Child Psychology, 17,* 455–471.

Reis, (1974). Central neurotransmitters in aggression. In S.H. Frazier (Ed.), *Aggression* (Vol. 52, pp. 119–148). Baltimore: Williams & Wilkins.

Reiss, M.J. (1984). Human sociobiology. *Zygon Journal of Religion and Science, 19,* 117–140.

Rodning, C., Beckwith, L., & Howard, J. (1989). Characteristics of attachment organization and play organization in prenatally drug-exposed toddlers. *Development and Psychopathology, 1,* 277–289.

Roecker Phelps, C.E. (2001). Children's responses to overt and relational aggression. *Journal of Clinical and Adolescent Psychology, 30,* 240–252.

Rosen, K.H. (1998). The family roots of aggression and violence: A life span perspective. In L. L'Abate (Ed.), *Family psychopathology: The relational roots of dysfunctional behavior.* New York: Guilford Press.

Rule, B.G., Taylor, B., & Dobbs, A.R. (1987). Priming effects of heat on aggressive thoughts. *Social Cognition, 5,* 131–144.

Sanson, A., & diMuccio, C. (1993). The influence of aggressive and neutral cartoons and toys on the behavior of preschool children. *Australian Psychologist, 28,* 93–99.

Schaal, B., Tremblay, R.E., Soussignan, R., & Susman, E.J. (1996). Male testosterone linked to high school dominance but low physical aggression in early adolescence. *Journal of the American Academy of Child and Adolescent Psychiatry, 19,* 1322–1330.

Schonfeld, I.S., Schaffer, D., O'Connor, P., & Portnoy, S. (1988). Conduct Disorder and cognitive functioning: Testing three causal hypotheses. *Child Development, 59,* 993–1007.

Schulz, K.P. (2002). Neurobiological correlates of aggressive and disruptive behavior in clinically-referred boys. *Dissertation Abstracts International: Section B: the Sciences and Engineering, 62,* 6017.

Slaby, R.G., & Guerra, N.G. (1988). Cognitive mediators of aggression in adolescent offenders: I. Assessment. *Developmental Psychology, 24,* 580–588.

Spielberg, L., & Rutkin, R. (1974). The effects of peer versus adult frustration on boys of middle childhood. *Journal of Psychology, 48,* 813–838.

Strauss, M.B. (1994). *Violence in the lives of adolescents.* New York: W.W. Norton.

Suarez, M. (2002). Relational aggression: An analysis of early childhood indicators. *Dissertation Abstracts International: Section B: The Sciences and Engineering, 62,* 5395.

Szatmari, P., Boyle, M., & Offord, D.R. (1989). ADHD and Conduct Disorder: Degree of diagnostic overlap and difference among correlates. *Journal of the American Academy of Child and Adolescent Psychiatry, 30,* 219–230.

Szatmari, P., Reitsma-Street, M., & Offord, D. (1986). Pregnancy and birth complications in antisocial adolescents and their siblings. *Canadian Journal of Psychiatry, 31,* 513–516.

Teerikangas, O.M., & Aronen, E.T. (1998). Effect of infant temperament and early intervention on the psychiatric symptoms of adolescents. *Adolescent Psychiatry, 37,* 1070–1077.

Thomas, A., & Chess, S. (1977). *Temperament and development.* New York: Brunner/Mazel.

Thomas, A., Chess, S., & Birch, H. G. (1968). *Temperament and behavior disorders in children.* Oxford, England: New York University Press.

Volling, B.L., Mackinnon-Lewis, C., Rabiner, D., & Baraduran, L.P. (1993). Children's social competence and sociometric status: Further explanation of aggression, social withdrawal and peer rejection. *Development and Psychopathology, 5,* 459–483.

Walker, S., Irving, K., & Berthelsen, D. (2002). Gender influences on preschool children's social problem-solving strategies. *Journal of Genetic Psychology, 163,* 197–210.

Whiting, B.B., & Whiting, J.W.M. (1975). *Children of six cultures: A psychocultural analysis.* Cambridge, MA: Harvard University Press.

Wood, W., Wong, F.Y., & Chachere, J.G. (1991). Effects of media violence on viewers' aggression in unconstrained social interaction. *Psychological Bulletin, 109,* 371–383.

Chapter 8

FORENSIC ISSUES AND VIOLENCE PREVENTION PROGRAMMING

Julia M. Klco

Mark is a biracial child who has been "kicked out" of several preschools. He is in his third foster home, is verbally and physically aggressive toward his foster mother (kicks and hits her), loves guns and knives, smashes cars and toys in his play, has to be number one, is aggressive and hurtful toward animals, is fascinated with fire, talks about wanting to kill his cousin (tried by sitting on him), hits, kicks, and bites his teachers and peers, and is fascinated with wearing diapers. He recently exposed himself in school. His 15-year-old mother took him to child protective services when he was 12 months old and said she could no longer care for him. At that time she had a criminal record and a drug and alcohol problem. Mark is four years old.

Brian, a Caucasian child from an intact family has an IQ in the genius range. He also has "blobby" people living in his head. The people include family members, made-up characters, Jesus and the Holy Spirit. He believes he can fax his thoughts to others and control his environment with the "machines" in his head. One of these machines is a large computer screen upon which he solves complicated math problems. When he was three, he head-butted his infant sister and continues to make her his "target" on a daily basis, laughing when she is hurt. It is suspected that head butting his sister caused a bilateral subdural hematoma when she was only a few months old. Brian is six years old.

Mack, a biracial child, is in his third foster home and has had one psychiatric hospitalization. He has killed animals in the last two foster homes and has caused extensive damage to a heating system by urinating into it. He hit his foster sister in the head with a stick so hard that it caused a concussion. In his current foster home, he was observed to be staring at his foster mother in her bed at 4:00 A.M. while he was wearing a *Scream* (movie) mask. Prior to being removed from his biological parents, he observed chronic drug and alcohol abuse and domestic violence, including a stabbing. He recently revealed a history of sexual abuse. Mack is eight years old.

Molly, a Caucasian female, is in her 21st foster home. She was adopted at one time; however, a sibling in the adoptive home sexually abused her in a closet at gunpoint. The adoption was terminated, and she bounced from home to home. She has already been arrested for battery because she punched one of her foster mothers. Her diagnoses include Attention-Deficit/Hyperactivity Disorder, Bipolar Disorder, and Reactive Attachment Disorder. Molly is 12 years old.

The stories of Mark, Brian, Mack, and Molly may easily turn into the stories of Jay and Mike that follow. The statistics don't bode well for them. All of these children have significant negative indicators for delinquent and violent behavior. At the age of 12, Molly has already had her first arrest.

Jay, an African American male, is in the department of corrections for killing a 5-year-old girl when he was 13. He strangled her to death. He is schizophrenic. He has no family that visits, and his biological mother is a heroin addict. Jay is 15 years old.

Mike, a Caucasian adolescent, is in prison for domestic battery. He was abandoned by his mother and lived with his father, who abused drugs and alcohol. Mike was physically abused and became involved in drugs and alcohol when he joined a gang at the age of 13. While he was in the department of corrections, I mediated between Mike and an opposing gang member. Mike became agitated and threw a chair at the other gang member. It hit me instead, and Mike dropped to the floor in tears, curling into a fetal position. He hadn't meant to hurt me. I watched Mike fall into a fetal position and break into tears because he had finally made an interpersonal connection with someone and thought he had hurt the only person he felt cared about him. Mike is 16.

After spending 10 years in law enforcement, I returned to school to become a clinical psychologist. I never expected to be faced with horrors worse than I had seen in police work. There I was accustomed to seeing violent children who "knew their rights," but rarely did I have knowledge of their histories. I remember being disturbed at the number of runaways who came through the booking room but were never asked why the streets seemed safer than home. What I didn't see then was the pervasive mistreatment of children in our juvenile justice system and correctional institutions, and the horrible abuse and neglect suffered at the hands of their parents, while the greater community looked the other way. The process of the criminal justice system, while considered the so-called end of the line for community and school factions, is the beginning of a trail of administrative policy, procedures, and aversive conditions. The interventions of the psychologist are essential to the youth to successfully move through the criminal justice system.

As an intern in a juvenile department of corrections facility, I worked with young men ages 12 to 21, who had emotional difficulties so severe that they could not be with the general prison population. At this same facility, my supervisor informed me that the clinic director had kicked a child in the head while he was face down in handcuffs. It was made clear to the staff that it would be "handled" internally. A young man who broke his hand in multiple places after punching a wall was left without treatment for more than a day. At that same facility, unlicensed and minimally trained staff provided therapeutic intervention for the most disturbed children in the facility. Although a role of advocate is needed by the professional, the reality is minimally trained staffers (American Psychological Association Task Force, 1992).

THE PROBLEM OF JUVENILE AGGRESSION

Therapists and teachers who work with young children such as Mark, Brian, and Mack often wonder what they'll be like when they grow up. Juvenile aggression is one of the acting-out behaviors that has a relatively high degree of stability over time. The latest statistics reveal that children younger than 13 are involved in almost 1 in 10 juvenile arrests (Snyder, Espiritu, Huizinga, Loeber, & Petechuk, 2003). Compared with juveniles who become involved in delinquency in adolescence, very young delinquents are at greater risk of becoming chronic, serious, and violent offenders. However, few studies to date focus solely on children/adolescents who have committed violent crimes. Frequently our most accessible samples come from prisons and not from the community. Factor-analytic studies (Lipsey, 1992) have indicated both single and multiple underlying dimensions of deviance.

Preschool and kindergarten offer new opportunities for problems or the reinforcement of aggressive problems that were already present with siblings at home. In elementary school, problems such as truancy, theft, and association with deviant peers begin to emerge (Barkley, 1997). Research has shown that juvenile crime rates peak during after-school hours on school days. In fact, the rate of juvenile violence in the after-school period is four times the rate in the juvenile curfew period, that is, from 11:00 P.M. to 6:00 A.M. (Snyder 2003). This speaks to the value of after-school programs and interventions.

We know that children repeatedly exposed to violence have lower thresholds of impulse control, are poorer judges of impending violence, and more frequently overreact to perceived threats (Sternberg et al., 1993; Song, Singer, & Angln, 1998). Mack, the eight-year-old described earlier, already demonstrates this. This is not only a psychological manifestation of early experiences but a physiological one as well. Weiner and Hess (1987) advocated the thorough assessment of the juvenile in terms of medical, social, and educational history as well as neurological aspects. They explained that because trauma and abuse may alter the structural integrity of the brain, questions about head injury, blackouts, pathological intoxication, and a myriad of other neurological signs of disturbance needs to be evaluated (Shapiro, 1992; Weiner & Hess, 1987). New research in this area implicates childhood abuse as being linked with excess neuronal irritability, excess electrical irritability in the limbic system, a heightened hormonal response to stress, and diminished development of the left cortex and left hippocampus, as well as reduced size of the corpus callosum. Limbic irritability can lead to aggression and violence toward oneself or others. These abnormalities contribute to the development of mental illness and are rarely treated in the type of multisystemic format that would help remediate the negative sequelae (Weiner & Hess, 1987).

PATHOLOGY AND JUVENILE AGGRESSION

According to a report submitted to Congress by the Coalition for Juvenile Justice, it was reported that more than half of juvenile offenders have a mental illness. In fact an estimated 50–75 percent of juvenile offenders suffer from mental health problems. When looking at adult offenders it has been found that of those with mental illness, 32 percent of the men and 78 percent of the women had histories of past physical and/or sexual abuse and that 26 percent had spent time in foster homes.

A history of violence, childhood abuse, and neglect is associated with a significant impact on the likelihood of arrest for delinquency, adult criminality, and violence. African Americans are most negatively affected. African American youth are twice as likely to be arrested and seven times as likely to be placed in detention facilities compared with white youth. According to data released in 1999, minority youth constituted about 32 percent of the youth population in the country yet represented 68 percent of those in secure institutional environments (Olweus, 1989). A study by Maxfield and Spatz-Widom (1996), found that victims of physical abuse were most likely (21%) to be arrested for violent offenses as a juvenile or adult. They also found that almost two-thirds of African American victims of abuse and neglect had been arrested and one-third had been arrested for a violent offense.

CONFINEMENT OR INSTITUTIONAL DETAINMENT?

As opposed to research on criminal statistics and national crime information reporting, self-report studies find an even higher proportion of the juvenile population involved in delinquent behavior. The official records appear to underreport delinquency. Law enforcement officers often make judgment calls and station adjustments with juveniles and although many may encounter the legal system, fewer are formally charged with a crime. Juvenile officers often handle the matter, so to speak, between victim and offender, involving parents when possible.

Overall juvenile crime rates have been falling since 1995. However, more youths are being committed to adult prisons. Between 1980 and 1997 the number of juvenile female offenders implicated in murders remained essentially constant, while males were responsible for all the fluctuations in juvenile homicide between 1980 and 1997. Since 1998, female arrests for murder have been on the increase, while the rate for males has declined. During the period between 1980 and 1997, the majority (93%) of known juvenile homicide offenders were male. More than half, 56 percent, were black, and 70 percent of victims were killed with a firearm. Male offenders most often killed acquaintances (54%), and female offenders were more likely to kill family members (39%) (Snyder et al., 2003).

Disproportionate minority confinement remains problematic, with blacks and Hispanics overrepresented in detainee populations. Minorities are more likely to be arrested, held in jail, sent to court for trial, convicted, and given longer sentences than are white youth (Song, Singer, & Anglin, 1998).

A single set of national standards for juvenile detention and confinement facilities has yet to be adopted. The American Academy of Child and Adolescent Psychiatry Task Force on Juvenile Justice Reform, in October of 2001, recommended that national standards for detention and confinement facilities be adopted by states and that health and mental health components of standards should be subject to review by national medical organizations. In addition, they recommended that the standards meet the developmental needs of these children, and they adopted a position statement calling for an end to capital punishment for any individual who commits an offense at the time the individual is younger than 18 years old. This decision is consistent with prevailing developmental theory and research.

Three states—Connecticut, New York, and North Carolina—now allow anyone older than 16 to be tried as an adult. Ten states—Georgia, Illinois, Louisiana, Massachusetts, Michigan, Missouri, New Hampshire, South Carolina, Texas, and Wisconsin—now allow anyone older than 17 to be tried as an adult, and in 15 states it is no longer up to a judge to decide whether a young person goes to adult court; it is the prosecutor's decision. In all 50 states there is at least one mechanism allowing people under 18 to be tried as adults under special circumstances.

TIMING OF INTERVENTION WITH AGGRESSIVE JUVENILES

There are few existing programs within the juvenile justice system to screen or help mentally ill youth. While there is so-called intervention, there is little treatment that actually occurs. State budgets are strained by the high cost of incarceration, and treatment programs, if they exist, are often the first to go. As an example, at the time of this writing the state of Illinois faces a 5 billion dollar budget deficit, and programs advocating for special needs children have already been cut. Some departments with the Department of Children and Family Services have seen up to a 75 percent reduction in staff, and there are no fewer children entering the system. In fact, the numbers as well as the horrors are increasing.

A TREATMENT EXAMPLE

DuPage County, one of the richest counties in Illinois, is making strides toward providing multisystemic intervention to their juvenile probation population. Despite these efforts, the probation department is contracting with doctoral-level therapists at less than half the usual and customary rate. This reimbursement rate is not likely to draw the best and the brightest in the field to work with the most disturbed youth. Unfortunately, it is feared that this may be the norm rather than the exception.

Overall, children in structured multimodality treatment programs show considerable improvement as compared to controls (Palmer, 2002). Some researchers indicate that the diagnosis and treatment of abuse and neglect can be viewed as a form of crime prevention (Maxfield & Spatz-Widom, 1996). The link between child maltreatment and juvenile offending is clear. With states cutting funding to protective services organizations, we are likely to see an even greater increase in delinquency within this population. The fact that antisocial behavior in the first few years of life predicts later antisocial behavior and delinquency is a strong argument for implementing prevention efforts as early in a child's life as possible (Hirschi, 1969). Mack (in the earlier clinical example) and his foster family, who hope to adopt him, receive therapy three times a week, twice in his home and once a week in the office. The lead therapist also meets regularly with his school, his occupational therapist, and other treatment providers. It is hoped that in a secure home with good parenting and multimodal intervention, Mack will be one of the survivors. More research is needed to identify not only the risk but the resiliency factors for children.

RECOMMENDATIONS

The situation calls for a continued look at developmental sequences; ages at which causal factors are most salient; and influences on onset, persistence, and desistance. Although we have direction in these areas, we still have little understanding about their interaction and individual resiliency components. This makes it difficult at best to know when to intervene and to know empirically which interventions will be the most effective. Clinical judgment alone cannot guide us.

Some of the programs that appear to be working are mentoring programs, dispute resolution, peer mediation, social skills training, cognitive behavior therapy, behavior modification, and truancy prevention. Proven interventions include multisystemic therapy, functional family therapy, and developmental ecological family intervention (Sternberg et al., 1993). The key to reducing serious and violent offending lies with early prevention efforts aimed at high-risk youth and interventions with serious and violent juvenile offenders.

Interventions must include the micro- and macroenvironment of the child and his or her family. (See chapters 1 and 2 for more theoretical details on this.) Social settings for targeting interventions include schools, the neighborhood, employers, residential institutions, churches, and even playgrounds and sporting events. Delinquent children I have worked with have said over and over, "the only people who care about me get paid to do it." Early intervention is key to helping these children and their families avoid the negative patterns and problematic environments that contribute to delinquency and violence.

REFERENCES

American Psychological Association. (1978). Report of the task force on the role of psychology in the criminal justice system. *American Psychologist, 33,* 1099–1113.

American Psychological Association Task Force. (1992). The use of psychiatric diagnosis in the legal process. Washington, DC: American Psychological Association.

Barkley, R.A. (1997). Defiant children: A clinician's manual for assessment and parent training (2nd ed.). New York: Guilford Press.

Hirschi, T. (1969). *Causes of delinquency.* Berkeley, CA: University of California Press.

Lipsey, M.W. (1992). Juvenile delinquency treatment: A meta-analytic inquiry into the variability of effects. In T. Cook, Cooper, H., Cordray, D.S. (Ed.), *Meta-analysis for explanation: A case book.* New York: Russell Sage Foundation.

Maxfield, M.G., & Spatz-Widom, C. (1996). The cycle of violence. *Archives of Pediatric and Adolescent Medicine, 150,* 390–395.

Olweus, D. (1989). Prevalence and incidence in the study of antisocial behavior: Definitions and measurement. In M. Klein (Ed.), *Cross-*

national research in self-reported crime and delinquency. Dordrecht, Netherlands: Kluwer.

Palmer, T. (2002). Individualized intervention with young multiple offenders. New York: Routledge.

Shapiro, D. L. (1992). *Forensic psychological assessment: An integrated approach.* Boston: Allyn and Bacon.

Snyder, H. N., Espiritu, R. C., Huizinga, D., Loeber, R., & Petechuk, D. (2003, March). Prevalence and development of child delinquency. Child delinquency bulletin. Washington, DC: U.S. Department of Justice, Office of Justice Programs, Office of Juvenile Justice and Delinquency Prevention.

Song L., Singer, M. I., & Angln, T. M. (1998). Violence exposure and emotional trauma as contributors to adolescents' violent behaviors. *Archives of Pediatric Adolescent Medicine, 152,* 531–536.

Sternberg, K. J., Lamb, M. E., & Greenbaum C., et al., (1993) Effects of domestic violence on children's behavior problems and depression. *Developmental Psychology 29,* 44–52.

Weiner, I., & Hess, A. (1987). *Handbook of forensic psychology.* New York: Wiley.

Part III

BEHAVIOR EXPRESSIONS AND VIOLENCE PREVENTION PROGRAMMING

Chapter 9

RESEARCH ISSUES RELATED TO CONFLICT RESOLUTION INTERVENTION PROGRAMS

Kathy Sexton-Radek

With more than one-third of the deaths of children, adolescents, and young adults resulting from violence, intervention is essential (Gillock & Reyes, 1999; Lowry, Sleet, Duncan, Powell, & Kolbe, 1995). The causes of violence are multiple and complex, and they affect all segments of American society. Most commonly, factors such as poverty; unemployment; lack of educational opportunities; and access to drugs, alcohol, and firearms have been identified. Research design, by its feature of parsimony, makes difficult the development of sufficiently rigorous designs to measure intervention's effects on the various factors related to violence in youth. Also, design in this area of the literature is often used to describe the set-up strategies for administrative, educational, and legal approaches to combat violence. Race, ethnicity, income, and family structure provide some understanding of the expression of violence, but do not statistically predict violent expressions (Blum et al., 2000).

Table 9.1 represents this relationship. The top rankings are African American and Mexican males' deaths due to homicide. White, non-Hispanic males rank ninth in comparison to racial minorities with deaths due to homicide.

Parental supervision affects the expression of violence (Brendgen, Vitaro, Trenblay, & Lavoie, 2001). Dodge, Lochman, and Harnish (1997) reported in their findings that 15 percent of children engage in proactive aggression. This instrumental, offensive, so-called cold-

Table 9.1
YLL Due to Homicide by Race/Ethnicity and Gender, Chicago,
1993–1995

Group	Annual Avg. YLL	Rank*	% Total
NH black male	20,903	1	22.7
NH black female	4,035	4	8.3
NH white male	1,390	9	3.8
NH white female	460	9	3.0
Mexican male	3,328	1	24.1
Mexican female	296	5	5.2
Puerto Rican male	937	2	16.1
Puerto Rican female	138	6	5.8
All other people	32,131	1	14.2

*Rank of YLL (Years of Life Lost based on average age of 65 years; if homicide occurs, that age is subtracted from 65 to denote YLL) due to homicide compared to other causes.
Source: Illinois Department of Public Health (IDPH) Vital Records tapes. Reprinted from the *Chicago Violence Strategic Plan.*

blooded aggression *does not* require provocation or anger and is predictive of adolescent delinquency. This relationship has been found to be moderated by parental supervision (Brendgen et al., 2001). Adolescents exposed to recurring community violence experience psychological trauma. The focus here is in terms of the finding that violence is a stressful experience that requires psychological adaptation and that thus precipitates psychological symptoms (Rosenthal, 2000).

Olweus (1979) reviewed 16 studies of aggressive behavior. In this meta-analytic review, a substantial degree of stability over time for aggression was measured. A wide range of ages and intervals were studied. Teacher ratings and nominations as compared to peer ratings were found to be significantly correlated with aggressive behavior observations (Olweus, 1979). In Figures 9.1 and 9.2 the results of type of crime and offender age by rate in Chicago, respectively, are presented. The peak age with the most frequently occurring deaths, in both figures, is the 15 to 25 year cohort.

Other research in this area has examined the role of social support in mediating aggressive behavior. In one project, Zhang (1994) describes the role of social support in getting the students to recognize mutual needs and interest among school peers and family members.

Figure 9.1
Victim Age-Specific Rates for Selected Crimes, Chicago Occurrence, 1996

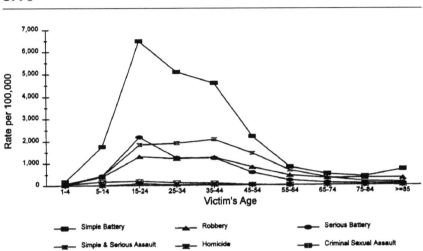

Furthermore, mutual relationships maximize resources to the students for achieving their goals. Johnson and Johnson (1994) identify that the scholarship environment includes controversy that prompts increased student achievement, critical thinking, higher-level reasoning, and intrinsic motivation to learn. With the cognitive/emotional buttress of social support, the psychologically isolated student may express reactive aggression in other ways.

Figure 9.2
Risk of Being a Violent Crime Offender against Children Younger than 13 Years, Chicago Occurrence, 1996

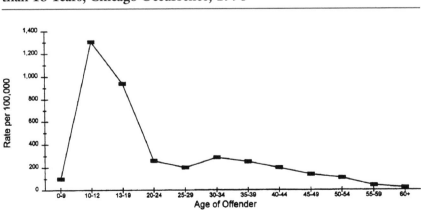

LONGITUDINAL STUDIES OF VIOLENT BEHAVIOR

In this representative review, studies examining the stability over time of violence expression are examined. Schwab-Stone, Cheng, and Greenberger (1999) identify the need to consider individual differences in the effects of violence exposure. In their examination of 2,885 urban 6th-, 8th-, and 10th-grade students of a community sample, exposure to violence was found to be associated with adolescents' externalizing behavior and internalizing symptoms. Both the extent of exposure to violence and the stability of externalizing and internalizing behaviors were significant. Schwab-Stone et al. (1999) comment that their findings indicate that over a two-year interval violence was substantially associated with internalizing and externalizing symptoms. Dishion and Andrews (1995) targeted parents' use of effective and noncoercive family management practices. Reports of reduced drug use and improvement in school by at-risk adolescents prompted the consideration of this factor as affecting expression of violence. Dishion and Andrews (1995) reported beneficial effects on behavior problems in school by those students with parents involved in an intervention psychoeducation group.

In a process-oriented action research investigation, Carruthers, Sweeney, Kmitta, and Harris (1996) identified the need to examine how students in conflict resolution groups change during the course of the intervention. The effects of conflict resolution programs or academic performance, although important to identify, have not been examined.

Keltikangas-Järvinen (2001) followed children identified as aggressive for seven years. The results from this investigation using social skills measurements showed the stability of aggressive behavior in children. Bierman and Wargo (1995) followed sixth-grade boys identified as having aggressive behavior. The factor of social rejection differentiated the groups of aggressive boys from aggressive-rejected children exhibiting more conduct problems. Johnson and Johnson (1994) conducted a multisite, global study of conflict resolution tracing. In the group comparison from pre- to postintervention, the students demonstrated their learning and application of the material.

Keltikangas-Järvinen and Pakasiahti (1998) reported results from a seven-year follow-up study from childhood to late adolescence. Findings were reported in terms of whether or not problem coping strategies developed, in order to distinguish whether the students behaved aggressively.

ASSESSMENT

Raters and Observers

Loeber, Green, Lahey, and Stouthamer-Loeber (1991) indicate that the identification of childhood disruptive disorders varies by rates and region. In their study of parent, teacher, and child ratings, they found the most consistency with severe, serious conduct problems. In that grouping, however, the child ratings differed in terms of the number of events—the children underestimated.

School psychologists rate schools, in general, as high in violence by location—urban inner-city, as compared to urban but not inner-city, suburban, and rural (Furlong, Babinski, Poland, Muñoz, & Boles, 1996). In a survey of 726 public school students in grades 7 through 12, it was reported that 1 in 5 live in a neighborhood with some crime. Males and those with low academic achievement were most likely to have committed acts of violence (Everett & Price, 1995). In a report by the National School Boards Association titled "Violence in the Schools: How America's School Boards Are Safeguarding Our Children," 78 percent of schools reported student assaults on students and 39 percent of urban districts reported a shooting or knifing in their schools (National School Boards Association, 1993).

Offord, Boyle, and Racine (1996) compared checklists of parents and teachers of children's violent behaviors aged 6 to 16 years. The parent-teacher agreement was low. Informant-specific phenomena are suggested. Power, Andrews, Eiraldi, Doherty, and Ikeda (1998) suggest the use of single versus multi-informant in terms of differentiating severe behavior problems and identifying the manifestations of aggressive behaviors, respectively. Hart, Lahey, Loeber, and Harrison (1994) address criterion-related validity of informants' ability to identify aggressive behaviors with a clinic-referred sample of boys aged 7–12 years. No associations were determined in this study; they concluded that a multi-informant diagnostic assessment is necessary to resolve the dilemma.

Curriculum Issues

Since the Public Health announcements, educators have tried to integrate conflict resolution (CR) knowledge and skills into their curriculums. As in all good teaching, so-called teachable moments that occur regularly, rather than a planned infusion into the curriculum of conflict resolution skills, are preferred by teachers. This issue of how and when CR should be taught received much attention from educators. Patterson (1995) indicated that state legislators have implemented laws requiring CR programming in the states of Ohio, South Carolina, and Texas. Such directives provide a means of introducing what some have called the fourth R into the curriculum.

Prescriptive, behavioral approaches to curricular design promote the specific planning and sequence of conflict resolution lessons. Goals and related objectives are specified. Accordingly, learning activities direct the students to adapt their knowledge, skills, and ability to affect conflicts they encounter. Other approaches strive to infuse conflict resolution lessons within the curriculum. In this manner, broad and general principles of conflict resolution are addressed by various subject matter and knowledge sets.

Finally, another curricular issue in the literature that frames the studies in this area is the design of the content. Curricular decisions become those of theoretical, practical, or both approaches. Some school districts develop their own curricula. There are also consultant design curricula and commercially produced curricula sold through professional conferences. Within the context of this issue is the means of implementation. In an attempt to establish a relationship between risk and protective factors, Dunham and Weaver (2002) surveyed undergraduates on their history of violent behaviors and demographic information. The researchers propose that identifying youth at risk for violence, rather than an entire population (i.e., school) or various subpopulations, is essential for directing intervention strategies.

Statistical information documents the problem of violence in the schools. Relevant questions about the nature of the problem, who is involved, who is affected, what interventions (i.e., CR curricula) are needed, and what works, need to be answered. In so doing, a multifaceted approach should be developed that accounts for the complexity of this youth violence.

Assessments such as those listed in Table 9.2 are useful for a variety of objectives. First, a needs assessment using one or more measures will help to identify the needs that can be addressed with responsive curricular planning. An important second objective with assessment is the identification of risk factors present in a group/school. Table 9.2 is also notable for the educator-practitioner because it presents a diverse resource of practical assessment tools that can be implemented in conflict-resolution-training programs.

Table 9.2
Survey Instruments

Teacher Ratings of the Violent Behavior of Students
    Aggression Behavior-Teacher Checklist
    Children's Behavior Questionnaire
    National School Crime and Safety Survey: Staff Form
    New York Teachers Ratings Scale
    School Behavior Checklist
    Social Behavior Questionnaire
Parent Ratings of Aggressive and Violent Behavior of Their Children
    Behavioral Assessment System for Children: Parent Ratings Scale
    Child Behavior Checklist: Parent Form
    Conner's Parent Ratings Scale
    Personality Inventory of Children
    Preschool and Kindergarten Behavior Scale
    Revised Louisville Behavior Checklist
    Self-Control Ratings Scale
Measures for School Counselors and Psychologists
    Fears and Worries Student Questionnaire
    The Hopelessness Scale for Children
    Preschool Behavior Questionnaire
    Wisconsin Aggression Behavior in Schools Survey
Student Self-Reports of Violence, Aggression and Anger
    Adolescent Violence Survey
    The Aggression Inventory
    The Aggression Questionnaire
    Buss-Durkee Hostility Inventory
    Multidimensional Anger Inventory
    Multidimensional School Anger Inventory
    Personality Inventory for Youth
    Social Skills Rating System
    State-Trait Anger Expression Inventory
    Weinberger Adjustment Inventory
    Youth Risk Behavior Survey
Peer Nominations of Violence and Aggression
    Peer Nomination Inventory
    Pupil Evaluation Inventory
Weapons
    Attitudes Toward Guns and Violence Questionnaire
    Tulane University National Youth Study
Measures of Community Violence
    The Children's Exposure to Community Violence Survey
    The Children's Report of Exposure to Violence
School and Community Risk Factors
    MacArthur Neighborhood Study
    The Oregon School Safety Survey
Measurements of Gangs and Attitudes Toward Gangs
    Attitudes Toward Gangs
    National Youth Gang Survey
Measures of Relationship Violence
    Acceptance of Couple Violence
    Perpetration in Dating Relationships
    Victimization in Dating Relationships

Source: Minogue, Kingery, and Murphy (1999).

DESIGN ISSUES

A varied number of applied field designs have been used in the measurement of CR outcomes. Rarely have true experiments been used, and infrequently have quasi-experimental designs been conducted. In fact, data collection has been described in terms of formative and summative approaches. In the formative design, modifications are made along the way. The perception of participants and educators of CR interventions are collected; the useful information gained in this format allows for a clearer understanding of the process of the intervention

With summative approaches, an applied field study procedure is conducted. Some collection of the changes and achievements of the CR interventions are done. In addition, qualitative approaches such as focus groups, naturalistic observation, and interviews add to the understanding of the CR intervention. Although it is traditional to conduct studies using a comparison or control group, designs applied to the field often offer a service to the participant, in this case CR skills, that are unethical to deny. Also, some argue that implementing an intervention without knowing its effects is unethical. A resolution is selective implementation of interventions and assessment.

Violence begets violence. It is often identified by antecedents to this behavior. A wide-angle focus brings into view the concept of risk factors. It seems that risk factors are subject to individual differences and social development. That is, some may show as a warning sign of latter violence, while the same risk factors may represent aberrant, developmentally immature behavior. A zoom lens perspective requires the matching of programs to identified risk factors in youth. Table 9.3 lists some common indicators of risk factors linked to school violence. It is suggested that applying the combination of resources from Table 9.2 to investigate Table 9.3 would provide an adequate needs assessment to construct a conflict resolution program. In fact, Paul (chapter 4) clearly describes the need to assess for psychopathology for an effective, impactful design of conflict resolution programming.

APPLIED RESEARCH ISSUES WITH CR INTERVENTION

The complicated situation of violent behaviors warrants multifaceted assessment. When applied, such methods yield valuable informa-

Table 9.3
Common Risk Factors Linked to School Violence

Community Characteristics
    Unemployment and underemployment of adults and youth
    Involvement of youth in violence in the community

Family Characteristics
    Family poverty
    Parents' education
    Effective discipline within the family
    Parental substance abuse

School Climate
    Safe and secure school environment
    Degree to which students are insulted or humiliated by school teachers or administrators

Substance Involvement
    Prevalence, frequency, and incidence of substance abuse
    Drug trafficking in schools and student involvement in drug trafficking in the community

Student Engagement at School
    Desire to do well or improve academically
    Extent of student alienation

Occurrences That Instigate Violence
    Recent abuse
    Recent victimization
    Insult
    Disrespect
    Dare other children to do things
    Name-calling

Attitudes Favoring Violence
    Admiring people who know how to fight with their fists (no weapons)
    Believing people should defend themselves or those they care about at all costs
    Enjoying fighting and/or hurting others

Weapon Possession at School or on School Grounds
    Knife
    Gun
    Bat or club
    Explosives
    Gang involvement in gun procurement

Source: Minogue, Kingery, and Murphy (1999).

tion about the nature of the youth's violent expressions. In turn, methods to measure the utility and effectiveness of CR interventions will determine the extent of the outcomes. In field settings, control or comparison group designs are difficult. Obtaining adequate sample sizes, sampling procedures within ethical standards, the measurement process, and intervention itself—while useful, these steps may circumvent the ability to study some populations to the extent that is needed. In applied field designs, typically, an assessment and postintervention measurement are done. Some studies emphasize their rigor with standardized assessments or the inclusion of psychometric testing of surveys used in the study.

The following review represents an analysis of representative research of CR curriculum. Several underlying themes are present in this literature. They are severity of violence expression; use of standardized measures; multifaceted assessment that includes teacher, parent, and child ratings; postintervention testing; and programmatic recommendations.

The review is presented to highlight the current status in this literature. This functional analysis of CR curriculum studies will provide the reader with a sample of the empirical knowledge in CR curriculum.

Table 9.4 depicts a representative sampling of participants ranging from elementary school, junior high school, high school, and community settings. The measurement instruments varied from self-report measures of conflict offered commercially, to research forms. The remarkable creativity in terms of design implementation in the often difficult-to-study field situations is represented by traditional factorial design to quasi-experimental designs of so-called one shot measurement/observation. Accordingly, this continuum of experimental design rigor yielded from specific to general conclusions. A tally across the 14 representative studies indicated positive qualitative findings such as "students learned the intervention" to measured, statistically significant changes in self-reported awareness and knowledge of coping skills to manage conflict.

Based on the review of the literature in CR interventions, a fundamental gap from experimental and quasi-experimental design is noted. In Wallace's (1971) work about scientific investigations, he stated that theories lead to hypotheses, then observations, then empirical investigations. Within this framework, this area of the literature is at the observation point (see Figure 9.3). Several key actions in the area need to occur for a movement to empiricism, where conclusions can be induced. A complete discussion of decision making about program evaluation design is contained in Harrell (1996).

Intervention differences are seen in terms of their focus on attitude or behavioral change. Those that focus on awareness and knowledge changes purport changes in attitude as a function of education CR program approaches. Behavioral change is more often reported in studies using standard measures in a planned manner and often a comparison group. An added bonus is the opportunity for participants to enact the skill training they are receiving.

What needs to happen?

- Central concepts are not defined. Are theories being considered?
- Rationale for the selection of a particular CR curriculum intervention needs to be determined.
- Training of CR leaders needs to be made uniform.
- The duration of CR needs to be clear.
- What is CR curriculum aimed at: children's knowledge, skills, abilities?
- Rationale for subject selection needs to be determined.
- Benefits to students, if any, are not identified.
- Study of both session/class and infusion approaches of CR curriculum needs to be undertaken.
- Consent forms and assent forms need to be stated.
- Statistical significance does not mean substantive significance.

Once issues of assessment are clearly indicated, those that address the need for a CR curriculum design for measurement or outcome will follow. Elements of the program such as staffing and type and amount of data that can be collected are key to the extent of a design. It is the identification of youth at risk and the provision of age-appropriate content that is consistent that will impact the success of the program. A design that takes these features into account is essential. The feasibility of the research plan will represent a trade-off between the resources for the project and design adherence. In applied studies such as investigations of CR curriculum, the trade-off is always one of external validity to precision of design choice and implementation. In effect, many completed studies in this area of the literature will advance this process with a focus to more precise direct measurement rather than summative/qualitative approaches. When the aforemen-

Table 9.4
Applied Research of CR Interventions

Authors	Sample	Measure	Design	Conclusions
Stevahn, Johnson, Johnson, & Real (1996)	111 7th & 8th graders K-8 public, Canada	How I manage Conflicts Measure Conflict Scenario Written Measure Conflict Word Association Measure	2 X 2 Factorial Design Random Assignment	Students learned the intervention Training enhances performance
Cirillo et al. (1998)	50 9-12 graders	Achievement tests Student Health Survey Demographic Survey	Pre test, Post test, following with comparison group	Treatment should be targeted at the intellectual level of the students Significant findings for educative approach
Stoolmiller, Eddy, & Reid (2000)	12 schools, 1-5th grade classrooms	Observation of aggressive behavior	Two group pre to post intervention design	Low reliability of observed behavior
Moriarity, Kalill, & Benander (2000)	Constituencies of the school	Presentation of violence data	One to three meetings	Educative approach to identify the early warning signs.
Zimmerman (1996)	12-24 year-olds at risk for violence	Television/Video presentation	Focus group sessions	Role of television via public service announcements
Carroll, Herbert, & Roy (1999)	Three Canadian high schools with noon-hour discussion and TV talk show	Questionnaire Call-ins from viewers	One shot	Change in awareness to violence
Goldberg (1999)	26 third graders compared to a second section of third graders	Vignette recordings	Comparison group with post test comparison	Measurement of children's cognition level necessary for acceptable CR planning

Study	Sample	Measure	Design	Findings
Paul, Sexton-Radek, Adickas, & Fousek (1999)	9th graders Urban public high school	Questionnaire How I Cope TOPSS	Program evaluation	Six week session of conflict resolution training heightens awareness, knowledge of coping skills
O'Donnell, Sandoval, & Duran (1998)	972 7-8th graders Urban public high school	Self-Report	Pre test–Post test Control group	10 session unit focused on violence prevention group differences in those that did service Emphasis multi-component violence prevention program
Lumsden (1994)	Mandated and self-selection	No measure	One-shot, no measurement	9 week CR class
Dudley, Johnson, & Johnson (1996)	176 students grades 6-9 Midwestern suburban middle school	"My Mediator" Notebook Recordings Experimenter's Ratings	Pre/post Experiential/Control	Improvement in negotiation skills for experiential group
Johnson, Johnson, Dudley, Mitchell & Fredrickson (1997)	198 6-9th graders	"My Mediator" Notebook recordings Perspective reversal procedures	Pre/post Experiential/Control	Knowledge of negotiation skills
Ashman & Conway (1993)	147 4-7th graders	Teacher ratings Trail Making Test Mages Test Plan Development	Assessment Study	Teacher ratings indicated process-based instruction led to positive changes in their teaching approaches and learning outcomes
Stevahn, Johnson, Johnson, Laginski, & O'Coin (1996)	42 9th graders	Reading and writing assignments	Pre/Post Experiential/Control Study	

Figure 9.3
The Wheel of Science

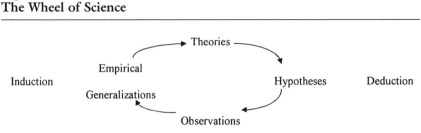

Source: Reprinted with permission from the *The Logic of Science in Sociology,* by Walter L. Wallace, p. 18. Copyright 1971 by Walter L. Wallace. Published by Aldine de Gruyter, Hawthorne, New York.

tioned needs are addressed, this area of research may be able to advance to another scientific level. Although accurate measurement and meaningful conclusions to conflict resolution programming are the metagoals, the impact of enacting change with violent youth in school settings is the essence.

REFERENCES

Anderson, E. (2002, December 1). Children need security: Professor. *Chicago Tribune.*

Ashman, A. F., & Conway, R. N. F. (1993). Teaching students to use process-based learning and problem solving strategies in mainstream classes. *Learning and Instruction, 3,* 73–92.

Bierman, K. L., & Wargo, J. B. (1995). Predicting the logintudinal course associated with aggressive-rejected, aggressive (non-rejected) and rejected (non-aggressive) status. *Development and Psychopathology, 7,* 669–682.

Blum, R., Beuhring, T., Shew, M., Bearinger, L., Sieving, R.E. & Resnick, M.D. (2000). The effects of race/ethnicity, income, and family structure on adolescent risk behaviors. *American Journal of Public Health, 90*(12), 1879–1884.

Bowen, N., & Bowen, G. (1999). Effects of crime and violence in neighborhoods and school behavior and performance of adolescents. *Journal of Adolescent Research, 14*(3), 319–342.

Brendgen, M., Vitaro, F., Tremblay, R., & Lavoie, F. (2001). Reactive and proactive aggression: Predictions to physical violence in different contexts and moderating effects of parental monitoring and caregiving behavior. *Journal of Abnormal Child Psychology, 29*(4), 293–304.

Carroll, G., Herbert, D., & Roy, J. (1999). Youth action strategies in violence prevention. *Journal of Adolescent Health, 25*(7), 6–13.

Carruthers, W., Sweeney, B., Kmitta, D., & Harris, G. (1996). Conflict resolution: An evaluation of the research literature and a model for program evaluation. *School Counselor, 44*(1), 5–18.

Chase, K., Treboux, D., O'Leary, D., & Strassberg, Z. (1998). Specificity of dating aggression and its justification among high-risk adolescents. *Journal of Abnormal Child Psychology, 26*(6).

Cirillo, K., Pruitt, B. E., & Colwell, B., (1998). School violence: Prevalence and intervention strategies for at-risk adolescents. *Adolescence, 33*(130), 319–330.

Dodge, K. A., Lochman, J. E., & Harnish, J. D. (1997). Reactive and proactive aggression in school children and psychiatrically impaired chronic assaultive youth. *Journal of Abnormal Psychology, 106*(1), 37–51.

Dishion, T., & Andrews, D. (1995). Preventing escalation in problem behaviors with high-risk young adolescents: Immediate and 1-year outcomes. *Journal of Consulting and Clinical Psychology, 63*(4), 538–548.

Dudley, B., Johnson, D. W., & Johnson, R. (1996). *The impact of conflict resolution training in a middle school on students' ability to engage in integrative negotiations.* Minneapolis: University of Minnesota, Cooperative Learning Center.

Dunham, K., & Weaver, S. R. (2002). Predictors of a new typology of youth violence. *Psi Chi-Journal of Undergraduate Research, XX,* 3–12.

Everett, S., & Price, J. (1995). Students' perceptions of violence in public schools: The Metlife Survey. *Journal of Adolescent Health, 17,* 345–352.

Furlong, M., Babinski, L., Poland, S., Muñoz, J., & Boles, S. (1996). Factors associated with school psychologists' perceptions of campus violence. *Psychology in the Schools, 33,* 28–37.

Gillock, K., & Reyes, O. (1999). Stress, supports and academic performance of urban, low-income, Mexican American adolescents. *Child Psychology, 28*(2), 259–282.

Goldberg, P. (1999). Increasing problem solving through metacognitive skills of planning, monitoring, and evaluating. *Research Report: Spencer Foundation, 43,* 1–23.

Harrell, W. A. (1996). The effects of shopping cart design and prior behavioral history on children's standing in cart seats. *Accident Analysis and Prevention, 28*(3), 385–389.

Hart, E., Lahey, B., Loeber, R., & Harrison, K. (1994). Criterion validity of informants in the diagnosis of disruptive behavior disorders in children: A preliminary study. *Journal of Consulting and Clinical Psychology, 62*(2), 410–414.

Johnson, D., & Johnson, R. (1994). Constructive conflict in the schools. *Journal of Social Issues, 50*(1), 117–137.

Keltikangas-Järvinen, L. (2001). Aggressive behavior and social problem-solving strategies: A review of the findings of a seven-year follow-up from childhood to late adolescence. *Clinical Behavior and Mental Health, 11,* 236–250.

Keltikangas-Järvinen, L., & Pakasiahti, L. (1998). Development of social problem-solving strategies and changes in aggressive behavior: A 7-year follow-up from childhood to late adolescence. *Aggressive Behavior, 25,* 269–279.

Loeber, R., Green, S., Lahey, B., & Stouthamer-Loeber, M. (1991). Differences and similarities between children, mothers, and teachers as informants on disruptive child behavior. *Journal of Abnormal Child Psychology, 19*(1), 75–95.

Lowry, R., Sleet, D., Duncan, C., Powell, K., & Kolbe, L. (1995). Adolescents at risk for violence. *Educational Psychology Review, 17*(1), 7–39.

Minogue, N., Kingery, P., & Murphy, L. (1999). *Approaches to assessing violence among youth.* Rosslyn, VA: The Hamilton Fish National Institute on School and Community.

Moriarty, A., Kalill, P., & Benander, M. (2000). The protocol approach to school violence. *Smith College Studies in Social Work, 71,* 279–381.

Offord, D., Boyle, M., & Racine, Y., Szatmari, P. (1996). Integrating assessment data from multiple informants. *Journal of the American Academy of Child Adolescence Psychiatry, 35*(8), 1078–1085.

Olweus, D. (1979). Stability of aggressive reaction patterns in males: A review. *Psychological Bulletin, 86*(4), 852–875.

Patterson, C. J. (1995). Developmental patterns of childhood peer relations as predictors of externalizing behavior problems. *Development and Psychopathology, 7*(4), 825–843.

Paul, P., Sexton-Radek, K., Adickas, J., & Fousek, B. (1999). The use of service learning to promote understanding of gang-related issues faced by adolescents. *NSEE Quarterly,* 3–7.

Power, T., Andrews, T., Eiraldi, R., Doherty, B., & Ikeda, M. (1998). Evaluating attention deficit hyperactivity disorder using multiple informants: The incremental utility of combining teacher with parent reports. *Psychological Assessment, 10*(3), 250–260.

Rosenthal, B. (2000). Exposure to community violence in adolescence: trauma symptoms. *American Journal of Public Health, 35*(138), 271–284.

Schwab-Stone, M., Cheng, C., & Greenberger, E. (1999). No safe haven II: The effects of violence exposure on urban youth. *Journal of the American Academy of Child and Adolescence Psychiatry, 38*(4), 359–367.

Stoolmiller, M., Eddy, J., & Reid, J. (2000). Detecting and describing preventive intervention effects in a universal school-based randomized trial targeting delinquent and violent behavior. *Journal of Consulting and Clinical Psychology, 68*(2), 296–306.

Wallace, W. (1971). *The logic of science in sociology.* New York: Aldine de Gruyter.

Zhang, Q. (1994). An intervention model of constructive conflict resolution and cooperative learning. *Journal of Social Issues, 99*(116), 99–116.

Zimmerman, J.D. (1996). A prosocial media strategy: "Youth Against Violence: Choose to De-Fuse." *American Journal of Orthopsychiatry, 66*(3), 354–361.

AFTERWORD

In these times of violence, it behooves professionals to increase their knowledge and awareness of pertinent issues. As weapons and violent ways pervade our schools, we can reassert a unified, knowledgeable, peaceful solution.

Clear conceptualization of the issues allow the reader of this book to concentrate on the violence in schools situation. Details of the rates of victimization, emotional states, and perceptions of the world are explained from developmental, interpersonal, and cognitive perspectives. This affords the reader with dimensions from which to broadly consider the issues. The pathways to violence, as identified by research studies, begin with acts of aggression. The etiology to the start of a pathway then becomes essential to understanding the expression of violence. Psychoemotional immaturity, experiences of loss and conflict, and cognitive distortion, generally stated, are potent trigger factors to youth violence. In chapter 2, the reader is given the image of prototypical violent behavior within the context of interpersonal object-relations viewpoint. In so doing, the provocation, pathway, and consequence of their behavior(s) are expressed. Interestingly, the developmental markers underscored in chapter 1 become highlighted in the cognitive focus of chapter 3. The implications for treatment planning are made possible by the clear identification of cognitive mediation factors of violent behavior.

Evidence for what the health-care professional can activate for prevention of youth violence is diverse and definitive. One learns from the readings of chapters in part II to intercede. The interruption of the behavioral expression with programming prevents school disruptions, attenuates pathways to pathology, and deters long-standing personality styles of bullying. However, the right type and extent of programming necessary for success are yet to be determined—limitations in design formulation and implementation need to be reconciled with the use of applied quasi-experimental designs, as discussed in chapter 9. Appendix II offers a study of such an approach. The findings, though limited by sample size, imply an effect from the conflict resolution training. System management of violent youth, largely in terms of consequences to these behaviors, becomes a forensic issue. As in most complicated clinical situations, individualized approaches tailored to the needs of the individual and particular situation provide a workable solution.

In total, the chapters present a vision based on scholarly and clinical experiences with violent youth. From conceptualization issues, to enacted techniques and assessment of consequences, to measured approaches to impede violent youth, readers are given thoughtful, useful information to facilitate their work and planning.

Appendix I

WEB RESOURCES FOR VIOLENCE PREVENTION PROGRAMMING

Whether implementation is within a classroom, after-school program, or other youth-focused setting, there are many resources available regarding program development for selecting social/emotional learning or character education curriculums. Due to the vast amount of literature on the topic, it can be overwhelming to decide which curriculum to use. To that end, the Collaborative for Academic, Social, and Emotional Learning (CASEL) has compiled these resources in an on-line program library located at www.casel.org. This Web site's library offers a variety of links to books, curriculum, and other resources for teachers, mental health care professionals, program development coordinators, and so forth. Due to the efforts of the staff at CASEL, searching for curriculum ideas has become more efficient and less intimidating. Individuals seeking more information on such materials are encouraged to visit this Web site.

Bully B'ware Productions, www.bullybeware.com

Children and Adults with Attention-Deficit/Hyperactivity Disorder, www.chadd.org

Committee for Children, www.cfchildren.org

National Criminal Justice Reference Services, www.ncjrs.org

National Youth Violence Campaign, sponsored by the Association for Conflict Resolution and American School Counselor Association, www.violencepreventionweek.org

North Carolina State University, www.ncsu.edu

Office of Juvenile Justice and Delinquency Prevention, http://ojjdp.
ncjrs.org

Prevention Partners, www.preventionpartners.com

United States Department of Health and Human Services, Substance
Abuse and Mental Health Services Administration, National Mental
Health Information Center, www.mentalhealth.org

What Is Bullying?, www.enlight-atlanta.org

Appendix II

CASE STUDY: SELF-PERCEPTION OF ANGER CONFLICT RESOLUTION INTERVENTION AT A CHICAGO INNER-CITY SCHOOL—FOURTH-GRADERS

Kathy Sexton-Radek and Patrice Paul

Project Description: A conflict resolution training for fourth-graders was requested by the principal. Three classes of fourth-graders were given a social-skills–based intervention of six weeks (once a week) focused on conflict resolution of bullying. Students' perceptions of the intervention were assessed.

Findings: Seventy-eight fourth-graders completed demographic and self-report measures of their view(s) about the intervention. The conflict resolution intervention was administered once a week for six weeks using a multisensory approach. Each topic was presented, and students were to discuss and explain their understanding of the topic. An applied exercise was conducted, and a project for the small groups of students was assigned for the next class meeting. Topics included communication skills, anger management, assertiveness, problem solving, and expression.

An anger inventory of 35 statements that the students rated as 0 = Never to 1 = Always was administered at preintervention and postintervention. The survey is scored in terms of four scores: anger experience, hostility, destructive expression, and positive coping. A paired t-test comparison of these scores indicated a statistically significant difference for anger experience ($T = -25.12$, $p < .05$), hostility ($T = -15.57$, $p > .05$), and positive coping ($T = -1.704$, $p > .02$). In a one-way analysis of variance to compare the responses of the three classes of students at preintervention, the positive coping variable was statistically significant ($F = 6.419$, $p < .05$). At postintervention, the anger experience scores distinguished the three groups ($F = 9.202$. $p < .05$).

Conclusions: The intervention was successful from the students' point of view in that it heightened their awareness of their anger experience, hostility, and positive coping. Initially, the groups were slightly different in terms of positive coping with one class (influenced by teacher), demonstrating high levels of constructive coping. The students' perception of their anger experience after the intervention was elevated. The intervention seemed to sensitize the students to provocations and faulty assumptions they encountered and were aware of that lead to anger expressions. We think the multisensory approach to conflict resolution training for the problem of bullying was effective.

GLOSSARY

Aggression: Intentional injury or harm to another person, usually associated with frustration.

Bullying: Aggressive behavior (usually chronic) by a child or adolescent toward smaller and weaker peers for the purpose of gaining or regaining power and control, gaining emotional gratification or eliminating emotional discomfort, or gaining peer status or acceptance.

Hostile attributional bias: A deficiency in attributional skills that tend to make one prone to interpret others' benign actions as being hostile.

Overt aggression: A behavior that involves direct verbal or physical aggression.

Proactive (instrumental) aggression: A type of aggression that is highly organized, so-called cold-blooded, appetitive in nature, and characterized by little autonomic activation. This type of aggression is usually less emotional and driven by the expectation of reward.

Reactive (interpersonally hostile) aggression: A type of aggression typified by so-called hot-blooded anger, menacing hostile attacks, defensiveness in response to a perceived threat, and intensive patterned autonomic activation (physical agitation). This type of aggression is usually a frustration response, associated with a lack of self-control.

Relational aggression: A behavior that is motivated with the intention of significantly manipulating or causing damage to another person's relationships or feeling of inclusion by the peer group.

Self-concept: The way a person sees herself of himself holistically.

Self-esteem: An individual's overall and specific positive or negative self-evaluation.

Social competence: The matrix of social skills that permit someone to navigate successfully in social interactions and situations.

Temperament: Patterns of arousal and emotional response that represent consistent and enduring characteristics in an individual.

BIBLIOGRAPHY

Chaiken, M. (1998). Tailoring established after-school programs to meet urban realities. In D. Elliott, B. Hamburg, & K. Williams (Eds.), *Violence in American Schools: A new perspective* (pp. 348–375). New York: Cambridge University Press.

Christiansen, J., Christiansen, J. L., & Howard, M. H. (1997). Using protective factors to enhance resilience and school success for at-risk students. *Intervention in School and Clinic, 33,* 86–89.

Corvo, K. N. (1997). Community-based youth violence prevention: A framework for planners and funders. *Youth and Society, 28,* 291–316.

Dishion, T. J., French, D. C., & Patterson, G. (1995). The development and ecology of antisocial behavior. In D. Cicchetti & D. J. Cohen (Eds.), *Developmental psychopathology:* Vol. 2. *Risk, disorder, and adaptation* (pp. 421–471). New York: Wiley.

Dishion, T. J., & Patterson, G. R. (1997). The timing and severity of antisocial behavior: Three hypotheses within an ecological framework. In D. Stoff, J. Brieling, & J. Maser (Eds.), *Handbook of antisocial behavior* (pp. 205–217). New York: Wiley.

Dishion, T. J., Patterson, G. R., Stoolmiller, M., & Skinner, M. L. (1991). Family, school, and behavioral antecedents to early adolescent involvement with antisocial peers. *Developmental Psychology, 27,* 172–180.

Egeland, B., Carlson, E., & Sroufe, L. A. (1993). Resilience as process. *Development and Psychopathology, 5,* 517–528.

Elder, G. (1998). Life course as developmental theory. *Child Development, 69,* 1–12.

Eron, L. D., Gentry, J. H., & Schlegal, P. (Eds.) (1994). *Reason to hope: A psychosocial perspective on violence and youth.* Washington, DC: American Psychological Association.

Fowles, D. (1994). A Motivational Theory of Psychopathology. In: W. D. Spaulding. *Integrative views of motivation, cognition, and emotion.* Lincoln, NE: University of Nebraska Press.

Fowles, D., Sutker, P., & Goodman (Eds.) (1994). *Psychopathy and social personality: A developmental perspective.* New York: Springer.

Garbarino, J. (1992). *Children and families in the social environment.* 2nd ed. New York: Aldine de Gruyter.

Guerra, N. G., Attar, B., & Weisberg, R. (1997). Prevention of aggression and violence among inner-city youths. In D. Stoff, J. Brieling, & J. Maser (Eds.), *Handbook of antisocial behavior* (pp. 375–383). New York: Wiley.

Gullotta, T. P., Adams, G. R., & Montemayor, R. (Eds.) (1998). *Delinquent violent youth: Theory and interventions.* Newbury Park, CA: Sage.

Huesmann, L. R., Guerra, N. G., Miller, L., & Zelli, A. (1992). The role of social norms in the development of aggression. In H. Zumckly & A. Fraczek (Eds.), *Socialization and aggression* (pp. 139–151). New York: Springer-Verlag.

Hyman, L. A., & Perone, D. C. (1998). The other side of school violence: Educator policies and practices that may contribute to student misbehavior. *Journal of School Psychology, 36,* 7–27.

Loeber, R., & Farrington, D. P. (Eds.) (1998). *Serious and violent juvenile offenders: Risk factors and successful intervention.* New York: Russell Sage.

Marans, S., & Adelman, A. (1997). Experiencing violence in a developmental context. In J. Osofsky (Ed.), *Children in a violent world* (pp. 202–222). New York: Guilford.

McLaughlin, M. W., & Irby, M. A. (1994). Urban sanctuaries: Neighborhood organizations that keep hope alive. *Phi Delta Kappan, 76,* 300–306.

Murphy, J. J., & Duncan, B. L. (1997). *Brief intervention for school problems: Collaborating for practical solutions.* New York: Guilford Press.

Myles, B. S., & Simpson, R. L. (1998). Aggression and violence by school-age children and youth: Understanding the aggression cycle and prevention/intervention strategies. *Intervention in School and Clinic, 33,* 259–264.

Patterson, G. H. (1992). Developmental changes in antisocial behavior. In R. D. Peters, R. J. McMahon, & V. L. Quincey (Eds.), *Aggression and violence throughout the life span* (pp. 52–82). Newbury Park, CA: Sage.

Reppucci, N. D., & Woolard, J. L. (1999). Social, community, and preventive interventions. *Annual Review of Psychology, 50,* 387–418.

Sampson, R. J., & Laub, J. H. (1993). *Crime in the making: Pathways and turning points through life.* Cambridge, MA: Harvard University Press.

Whittaker, J. K., Schinke, S. P., & Gilchrist, L. D. (1986). The ecological paradigm in child, youth and family services: Implications for policy and practice. *Social Service Review, 60,* 483–503.

INDEX

Absent parent, 81
Academic environment, 96
Active listening, 26
ADHD (Attention-Deficit/
  Hyperactivity Disorder), 123
Adolescent-limited behavior, 26–27
Aggression, 6, 35, 37, 159; types
  of, 122
Aggressive, 73, 129
Altruistic dynamics, 38
Amoric, 44
Anger, 5
Anger inventory, 179
Antisocial conduct, 10
Applied field study, 164
Assessments, 162
At-risk children, 64
Attachment system, 5

Blos, P., 35
Bonding, 22–23
Brain power, 98
Bronfenbrenner, B., 30
Bullied, 111
Bullying, 8, 103, 104, 107, 112,
  121, 125, 131, 134

Clinical setting, 41
Coercive parenting, 15
Cognitive style, 79, 80
Commitments, 17
Comprehensive curricula, 23
Conduct Disorder (CD), 74, 123
Correctional facility, 147
Co-victimization, 12
CR (conflict resolution) curricu-
  lum, 161–62, 166–68
Criminal violence, onset, 3
Cross-cultural studies, 104
Cultural norms, 115–16
Curricular, 162

Depression, 79
Difficult temperament, 74
Direct reinforcement, 76
Discriminating cues, 59
Distinct profile, perpetrators, 61

Easygoing, 21
Executive (higher-order) function-
  ing, 126
Exosystem, 16
Experiential curricula, 23

Family environment, 56
Fatalism, 11
Friendship-making skills, 94

Gender, 110
Gender differences, 132

Handguns, 4
Homicide, 4
Hostile aggression, 6
Human aggression, 37
Hyperactive-impulsive type of
    ADHD, 77

Identity, 45
Identity formation, 28
Incidental teaching, 94
Infant temperament, 125–26
Instrumental aggression, 6
Internalizing, 113
Interpersonal Cognitive Problem
    Solving (ICPS) program, 98
IQ, 19
Irritability, 79

Juvenile detention, 149–50
Juvenile justice system,
    147, 150

Landmarks of adolescence, 42
Law enforcement, 146
Lethal attacks, 4
Locus of control, 128
Low socioeconomic status, 75

Macrosystem, 16
Mesosystem, 15
Microsystem, 15
Multisystematic intervention, 151

Nested social contexts, 14
Niche picking, 13

Oppositional Defiant Disorder
    (ODD), 74
Overt bullying, 104

Parental abuse, 77
Parental monitoring, 115, 157
Parents, 106
Peer victimization, 108, 110
Perpetrator(s), 51, 61, 95
Perspective taking, 134
Physical aggression, 81
Physical bullying, 52
Potential predators, 12
Prevention, 152
Primary prevention, 65, 66
Prisons, 147
Private practice, 103, 117
Prosocial attitude, 26
Prosocial behavior, 94

Quasi-experimental design, 166

Rational beliefs, 63
Reciprocal causation, 10
Relational aggression, 6
Relational bullying, 53
Resilient children, 20
Risk factor, 75
Rough justice, 28

Safety, 92
School-based, 135
School climate, 60
School safety, 55
School shootings, 92
School violence programs, 93, 95,
    96
Schools, 161
Secondary prevention, 66
Self-efficacy, 12
Self-preserving, 80
Self-righting mechanisms, 18

Skills, 26
Snares, 17
Social aggression, 107
Social and emotional learning
  (SEL), 83
Social conditioning, 133
Social cues, 58
Social development model, 22
Social-emotional, 40, 50
Social goals, 58
Social-information processing, 127
Social scripts, 13
Social support, 113
S-O-S (Skills-Opportunities-
  Sanctions) model, 23, 29
Street style, 7
Survey instruments, 163

Temperament, 125–26
Thematic curricula, 23

V Code, 36
Verbal bullying, 53
Victim-child, 105
Victimization, 4, 12, 56, 109, 110,
  113, 131
Vigilance, 59
Violence, 91
Violence prevention programs, 93,
  96
Violent acts, 5
Violent crimes, 147

Youth violence, 73, 92

ABOUT THE EDITOR AND THE CONTRIBUTORS

KATHY SEXTON-RADEK has a private practice in La Grange, Illinois, and is a licensed clinical psychologist. She has initiated and coordinated several service learning projects that entail the training of undergraduate and graduate students in the implementation of conflict resolution issues. She has completed postdoctoral training in the areas of clinical psychopharmacology and sleep medicine.

KORRIE ALLEN attended the University of Notre Dame, earning a bachelor of arts in psychology. Following Notre Dame, she earned a graduate assistantship to St. Johns University, where she obtained a master of science and doctorate in psychology. She completed her doctoral internship at the Albert Ellis Institute, and is currently working as a postdoctoral fellow at the Center for Pediatric Research in Norfolk, Virginia.

LYNDA BOCKEWITZ completed her undergraduate training at Elmhurst College in Elmhurst, Illinois, where she received a bachelor's degree with honor in psychology. She is currently a doctoral candidate in the Clinical Psychology Program at Jackson State University in Jackson, Mississippi. She completed her clinical internship at the University of Miami Medical Center/Jackson Memorial Hospital in Miami, Florida, with a specialization in child and adolescent psychology and pediatric behavioral medicine. She is currently an assistant professor of psychology at Blackburn College in Carlinville, Illinois.

Her research interests include school violence, child and adolescent psychopathology and treatment, and pediatric behavioral medicine.

JAMES GALEZEWSKI is the cofounder of the Center for Life Balance in Chicago. He received his degree in clinical psychology at the Chicago School of Professional Psychology. He has received extensive clinical training at Linden Oaks Hospital in Naperville and Resurrection Hospital in Chicago. He is also a member of the psychology faculty at Elmhurst College. Dr. Galezewski is a licensed clinical psychologist in the states of Illinois and Indiana, as well as a licensed marriage and family therapist in the state of Illinois. He specializes in executive coaching.

CHARLES E. GOLDSMITH is an ordained minister of the United Church of Christ. He received his doctorate in clinical psychology from Boston University. He is a practicing psychologist with 20-plus years of private practice work with youth and is a consultant at the Congregational Home in Wisconsin.

JULIA M. KLCO currently teaches as an adjunct professor at the Illinois School of Professional Psychology, Northwest Campus, and is a consultant to the forensic program. She has private practices in Wheaton and Rockford, Illinois, and has also published in the area of Munchausen's Syndrome by Proxy and Trauma and presents nationally on trauma across the age span. She credits a previous career in law enforcement as contributing significantly to her forensic and clinical work.

MARY LAWSON is a developmental psychologist whose interests cover the entire life span. She received a doctorate from the Committee on Human Development at the University of Chicago in 1985 and has taught at Northeastern Illinois University, St. Xavier University, and Elmhurst College. She is a member of the American Psychological Association.

AMY C. PATELLA is a clinical psychology intern and a doctor of psychology student at the Chicago School of Professional Psychology. Ms. Patella has worked as a high school teacher and a school-based psychotherapist. She is interested in organizational and school consultation, cross-cultural issues, and rites of passage.

PATRICE PAUL received her doctorate in clinical psychology from the Illinois Institute of Technology and completed her clinical training at the University of Chicago Hospitals. She is a licensed clinical psychologist with expertise in assessment and therapy, specializing in children and adolescents in both private and university settings. Dr. Paul also has experience teaching in the area of clinical psychology to both undergraduate and graduate students. She functions as a consultant to community action councils and schools regarding program development, and she provides workshops for parents and teachers on related topics.

RENE PICHLER has her doctorate degree from the Illinois Institute of Technology in Chicago, Illinois. Her research has focused primarily on the development of children. She enjoys growing in the field of psychology by teaching undergraduate psychology courses and working as a research assistant for a local hospital. Other research interests include sport and health psychology. Her professional affiliations include the American Psychological Association. Rene received her undergraduate psychology bachelor's degree from Elmhurst College in Elmhurst, Illinois.

THERESA RISOLO is a licensed clinical psychologist in private practice and a clinical supervisor for the Chicago School of Professional Psychology. Dr. Risolo has worked as a high school teacher, within the foster care system, and as staff psychologist in a child welfare agency. For over 20 years her clinical practice with children, adolescents, and adults has dealt directly with the issues of trauma that are the result of bullying behaviors. Dr. Risolo has testified as an expert witness in criminal trials on the effects of domestic violence. She is a frequent contributor to local newspapers and was prominent in a nationally televised MSNBC special on "Exorcism."

AMANDA URBAN is working at a postdoctorate at the University of Chicago. Past work experience includes teaching violence prevention classes in Chicago public schools, intermittent explosive disorder, practicum in psychotherapy, and assessment of adults and adolescents. Amanda's research interests include neuropsychological assessment, body image/women's health issues, sexual dysfunction, and psychotherapy with an adolescent population.

BOSTON PUBLIC LIBRARY

3 9999 05560 889 5

WEST ROXBURY BRANCH